Dancing about Architecture is a Reasonable Thing to Do

DANCING ABOUT ARCHITECTURE IS A REASONABLE
THING TO DO
Writing about Music, Meaning, and the Ineffable

Cascade Books
An Imprint of Wipf and Stock Publishers
199 W. 8th Ave., Suite 3
Eugene, OR 97401

www.wipfandstock.com

PAPERBACK ISBN: 978-1-4982-9382-2
HARDCOVER ISBN: 978-1-4982-9384-6
EBOOK ISBN: 978-1-4982-9383-9

Cataloguing-in-Publication data:

Names: Heng Hartse, Joel.
Title: Dancing about architecture is a reasonable thing to do : writing
about music, meaning, and the ineffable / Joel Heng Hartse.
Description: Eugene, OR: Cascade Books, 2022 | Includes bibliographical
references.
Identifiers: ISBN 978-1-4982-9382-2 (paperback) | ISBN 978-1-4982-9384-6
(hardcover) | ISBN 978-1-4982-9383-9 (ebook)
Subjects: LCSH: Popular music—History and criticism. | Musical criticism.
| Popular music—Religious aspects.
Classification: ML3470 H464 2022 (print) | ML3470 (ebook)

Dancing about Architecture is a Reasonable Thing to Do

Writing about
Music, Meaning, and the Ineffable

Joel Heng Hartse

CASCADE *Books* • Eugene, Oregon

For Sarah, who will probably not read this but without whom it would not have been written

. . . the art critic can never be epistemologically capable of describing art by thinking *at* being, but must think *from* and *within* being. I have thus deemed it a necessity to describe rock 'n' roll by allowing my description to be itself a parallel artistic effort.

—Richard Meltzer, *The Aesthetics of Rock*

It all has to do with it.

—John Coltrane, in the liner notes to *A Love Supreme*

Contents

CONTENTS

Acknowledgments

Thanks to editors and professors under whose auspices certain pieces here were written and ideas developed over the last twenty years or so, including Mary Kenagy Mitchell, Greg Wolfe, David Stacey, Tom Trzyna, Katelyn Beaty, Luke Reinsma, Mary Ann Creadon, Ted Olsen, Kate Shellnutt, Aaron Epp, Aiden Enns, Alan Noble, Patton Dodd, Corrie Mitchell, Jason Dodd, Hank Sims, Andrew David, Chris Keller, Hank Sims, and Luke Baumgarten.

Thanks to gracious readers, Chrindie heads, and friends like Mischa Willett, Jason Morehead, Alan Parish, Adrian Parrish, Ryan Ruppe, and literally everyone else who read the first book.

Thanks to musicians who had something to say back to me when I wrote something about them, including Torquil Campbell, Sally Ellyson, Dan Messé, Lee Bozeman, and Chris Foley.

Thanks to kindred spirits in making music mean, including Hedy Law, Matt Smith, Nathan Conant, Kevin Scott Davis, Matt Basinger, Andrew Best, and Daniel Boatsman.

Thanks to Ben and Ollie for many sing-alongs.

Thanks to Clare Sully-Stendahl for being incredibly good at tracking down original sources.

Thanks to Chris Spinks for letting me do this again.

Some portions of this book were first published in slightly differ-ent forms and are reprinted here with permission:

"Why Dancing about Architecture is a Reasonable Thing to Do" was originally published as "Making Meaning out of Music, or Dancing about Architecture is a Reasonable Thing to Do" in *Im-age,* Issue 86.

Some portions of "What Dancing about Architecture Does" were published in "Are Weezer's Songs from the Black Hole *Pinkerton* in Its Truest Form?" by *Popmatters,* on the web.

"How Not to Listen to Sufjan Stevens" was originally published as "How Not to Listen to the New Sufjan Stevens Album" in *Christi-anity Today,* on the web.

"Luxury: Transcendence and Transgression" was originally pub-lished as "Transcendence, Transgression, and Rock & Roll: The Music of Luxury" in *Christ & Pop Culture,* Volume 2, Issue 13.

A shorter version of the interview with Slim Moon was originally published online by *OnFaith,* which no longer exists.

"Old Time Bible House" was originally published in *North Coast Journal.*

"Ripping through Flesh, Wailing" was originally published in the *Inlander.*

"The Dears: Protest" was originally published online by *Bandop-pler,* which no longer exists.

"There is Only One Thing: Stars and the Soft Revolution" was originally published as "Stars: Set Yourself on Fire" in the *Other Journal*, on the web.

"Dance Dance Revolution" was originally published as "Ass-Shaking Great Awakening" in *Geez*, Issue 11.

"Rocking Out with the Weakerthans" contains elements of "Beyond the Pomo Blues with the Weakerthans," originally published by the *Other Journal*, on the web, and "The Weakerthans Make Strong Music," originally published by *Beliefnet*, on the web.

"Perfect Sound Forever" was originally published as "The Pitch Goes On" by the *Behemoth*, Issue 53, on the web.

"Groans Too Deep" contains elements of "Groans too Deep for Words," originally published in *Christianity Today*, and "The Worship-Ness of Sigur Rós," originally published by *Beliefnet*, on the web.

"World Wide Pants" was originally published by the *Inlander*.

Introduction

Criticism often feels like the wrong word for writing about popular music. I've written about music professionally (and unprofessionally) for twenty years, but even when I was regularly hustling for alt-weekly and magazine music-writing gigs, I struggled with what to call myself. "Music critic" felt and feels wrong, because I don't think most music writing actually jives with our pop culture's depiction of the critic, an elitist, cynical know-it-all who doles out bad reviews—like Anton Ego in *Ratatouille*,[1] or Andy Bernard in *The Office*[2] when he's contemplating a career change ("I could be a food critic: 'These muffins taste bad.' Or an art critic: 'That painting is bad.'"), or my personal favorite, *Futurama*'s[3] Dr. Zoidberg, who simply shouts at a symphony, "Your music's bad and you should feel bad!"

"Professional appreciator"—the term used by Rob Gordon, the protagonist of the venerable music-nerd film *High Fidelity*[4]— comes closer to what I think people who write about music are at heart. "Lover" is sometimes the best I can come up with. "Nerd" may be a close second. Both suggest a kind of helpless resignation, an admission that for some reason, and not necessarily a professional one, we are stuck doing this almost whether we want to or

1. Giacchino, *Ratatouille.*
2. Blitz, "Stress Relief."
3. Haaland, "The Devil's Hands are Idle Things."
4. Frears, *High Fidelity*, 1:38:07.

not, listening to and enjoying and being frustrated by and commenting on and writing about music.

For a while I had "writer-about-music" as my title in my email signature. It was at least more expansive, more in line with what I wanted to be, which is not primarily a *reviewer* of music or a *critiquer* of it, but someone who wants to exegete and explore every nook and cranny of pop music, from the sounds to the feelings to the economics to the sociology to the aesthetics, on and on, endlessly. For those of us already stuck in the pop music world, it matters very little what we call ourselves. We're going to be writing, reading, and thinking about music even if it doesn't make us any money or add any appreciable benefits to our lives. (And it won't, really, except for the occasional free concert ticket, which is not at all as exciting as it sounds.) I believe, I really do, that music is gloriously superfluous to survival, that it offers a surfeit of meaning and beauty that immeasurably enriches life. As the great songwriter Rich Mullins once said, "Of all things, music is the most frivolous and the most useless. You can't eat it, you can't drive it, you can't live in it, you can't wear it. But your life wouldn't be worth much without it."[5] There are many of us who need no convincing in this area. As they say on the internet: *if you know, you know.*

Music is one of many life-enriching cultural practices which, because it is so beloved, ends up having a whole discourse community built around it. For some people maybe it's food, or movies, or fashion, or technology. Whatever it is, if there's a subreddit or a thousand blogs or a newspaper column or a book about it, the people generating the discourse about it didn't seek a professional identity in That Thing We Nerd Out About first: it was always the love. We see something that makes an otherworldly, primal connection, and we think "Yes. This. More of this." And we start to try to figure out why that's happening and what the implications are and why it works differently for other people and why it is extremely important to, for example, explain the deeply beautiful and tragic arc of a relationship that plays out over the course of the last few Björk albums, or why the "Funky Drummer" sample

---

5. Mullins, quoted in Long, "O, To Be Rich."

endures, or how the syncopation works on that weirdly off-kilter Radiohead song. And we run with it, and we make more and more *stuff* about it. There is something that drives us not simply to *experience* these cultural practices and artifacts we love, and not even simply to *enjoy* them, but to *participate in and become part of them* even if we are not, strictly speaking, making them. But in fact, writing about music is, in a very real way, to make it, to participate in building a world where it matters. I take that Richard Meltzer quote from the epigraph as my mantra: writing about music is an activity that comes from the same place, mentally, emotionally, spiritually, socially, and cognitively, as making it.

Writing about popular music is, or it can be, so much more than "reviewing" songs or albums. At its best, writing about music illuminates the world. It's a deeply personal thing, a desire-driven, participatory creation. It's an excavation of the self. It's an autopsy of feeling. It's phenomenological autoethnography. It's an objective description of your subjective encounter with a transcendent experience. It's an act of meaning-making, of love, of self-disclosure, of self-giving, of communication, of meaning, of prayer, of worship. I see the desire to talk about music or write about it or understand it some way as part of the same creative and extravagant and maybe even religious impulse that is behind a lot of human activity: behind music, behind language, behind artmaking, behind love. There's this response to something ineffable, something you see and desire. I think that's part of who we are because of how this universe works.

This book is not an *argument* about any of this per se, but it is an attempt to unpack Meltzer's "parallel artistic effort" and/or Coltrane's "It all has to do with it" when it comes to writing about popular music. This book is arranged into two halves: the first section comprises three longer chapters exploring the *how*, *what*, and *why* of writing about pop music; the second is shorter pieces I have written over the last twenty years (most never before published, or published in magazines that no longer exist, or simply not widely read) that represent attempts to write about music that also approach big, difficult, and almost unwriteaboutable concepts like faith, hope, transcendence, loss, and the self.

In the first chapter, which attempts to explain *why* people write about music, before we even have much time to get warmed up, things get very meta as I write about books about writing about music and situate the whole enterprise as an act of faith in meaning-making. The second chapter examines *what* the enterprise of "music writing" in the pop music world entails, using the band Weezer as an example. The final chapter of the first section looks at *how* it is even possible to understand and "evaluate" popular music in the first place (spoiler alert: I don't think we "evaluate" it in the traditional sense of "criticism.") The second section includes short introductions to each sub-theme, so I will not touch on those here.

I am finishing this book in the fall of 2020, in the thick of the COVID-19 pandemic. As one of my favorite bands, Five Iron Frenzy, said in a single this year: "We are alive if we still sing." And, I would add, if we still write.

On Writing about Music

Why Dancing about Architecture
Is a Reasonable Thing to Do

Around the time I started getting paychecks for writing about music, I tried to read the dense and difficult book *The Aesthetics of Rock* by the rock-critic-cum-philosopher Richard Meltzer. I was unable to finish it, but a single sentence Meltzer wrote has both haunted and inspired me for years. Near the beginning of his book, Meltzer writes that "the art critic can never be epistemologically capable of describing art by thinking *at* being, but must think *from* and *within* being. I have thus deemed it a necessity to describe rock 'n' roll by allowing my description to be itself a parallel artistic effort."[1]

Like other aestheticians before him, Meltzer seems here to be critiquing the Kantian notion of disinterest as paramount to aesthetic judgment—the idea that to evaluate a work of art, the observer must maintain some degree of objective detachment. Today, I suppose many of us would think disinterest both impossible and undesirable; why would I not want to bring *myself* to my appreciation of art? How, indeed, could one not? But Meltzer goes a step further by describing writing about music as "a parallel artistic effort"—not an objective process of judgment done from afar, nor even a secondary, parasitic act of interpretation made possible only by a primary source, but, essentially, *the same thing*.

A lot of writing about music does not feel like "a parallel artistic effort." It feels like showy self-aggrandizement. I know this because I have done a lot of it myself. But the best writing about

1. Meltzer, *Aesthetics of Rock*, 7.

3

music that I know does feel as revelatory and true and beautiful as the best music that I know, and writing about music, at its best, feels essential to the experience of being a music listener—or music lover, really—itself.

So I agree with Meltzer, despite the existing corpus of music criticism that does feel alternately like straight-up shilling or just reciting secret passwords to the cool kids' club. I'd like to keep this idea of the parallel artistic effort in mind, and to make a more audacious claim: that making music, writing about music, and loving music are all parallel endeavors in the making of meaning, and that as manifestations of meaning-making, they are all, in a sense, the same endeavor, and that that endeavor is in fact essentially mysterious, even religious, an impulse as old as humanity itself. The idea, odd as it may seem to advance in a book about pop music, is that all human meaning-making endeavors are variations on a theme, and that theme is the transcendent, seemingly divine, ineffable *thing* that the Greeks and early Christians called *logos*. Call it what you will—this thing that drives humans to make art and language and music and all other forms of meaning. Rather than music criticism being a dry and parasitic exercise, or a patently absurd and impossible one, as some seem to think, it is in fact a product of a person's encounter with that deep-down meaning-making thing inside all of us.

It's been said, rather famously, that writing about music is like dancing about architecture. This aphorism has been attributed to Frank Zappa, Elvis Costello, Charles Mingus, Miles Davis, George Carlin, and Thelonious Monk, to name a few. Probably none of them said it; if you do enough digging on the internet you get the slightly unexciting likely truth that it was the comedian Martin Mull, sometime in the 1980s. Interestingly enough, though, the formula "writing about music is like [blanking] about [blank]" is about a hundred years old, according to a seemingly credible website called Quote Investigator, the author of which dug up an instance from the *New Republic* in 1918 which states that "writing about music is as illogical as singing about economics."[2]

2. H.K.M. "The Unseen World," 63, quoted in O'Toole, "Writing About Music."

However you formulate the quote, it's funny and cute, but also unimaginative and wrong. The implication is that one art form, or one creative act or meaning-making event, can't logically interpret another. How could lifeless ink on a page ever hope to capture the life and the movement of a melody? The short answer is that it could not, but this answer assumes that somehow it is *supposed to*. The punchline is that writing about music is not for *representing* music at all. It is, like music itself, an endeavor to *mean*.

And frankly, dancing about architecture is not so unthinkable, as long as we are comfortable with a looser definition of the word *about*. When we say a work (or an event, or anything we might interpret) is *about* something, we are usually eliding something ceaselessly complex. What is *The Great Gatsby* about? What is the Beatles' "A Day in the Life" about? The *Mona Lisa* or *Jurassic Park* or *A Love Supreme*? The question is too simplistic to answer. One ends up with an unsatisfying, static, CliffsNotes interpretation. A dance about architecture would not simply be an attempt to represent or explain or interpret a building: it could riff on, or build on, or be inspired by, or otherwise tangentially be related to a building, maybe. It would be a different thing, somehow related to what came before. It wouldn't be *impossible*. And of course, neither is writing about music.

The novelist Arthur Phillips puts it well in his defense of using music as a device in fiction:

> There is nothing inherently laughable or false about a dance about architecture. But you wouldn't want to forsake buildings to live in the dance, nor would I give up music in exchange for my favorite writers' descriptions of it. Yet there is a pleasure to be found in that dance, in that writing, that both invokes the subject and creates something new from it, and, when you return to the architecture, to the music, when you wander the halls or turn on your stereo, you carry with you now some new wisdom and love for the house, for the song, that you gained elsewhere.[3]

3. Phillips, "Dancing about Architecture."

Wisdom and love. Lofty goals for writing about music, or anything—but not impossible. Some might say that criticism by its nature is unlikely to inspire "love," since some people seem to view music criticism as a kind of creative vampirism in which those who can't do (writers) siphon some of the lively, honest-to-goodness art-making lifeblood of musicians. I disagree. At its best, the relationship of criticism to the arts themselves is one that binds together art and its interpretation. George Steiner's *Real Presences*—a book-length essay arguing against criticism and in favor of primary texts, and artworks, as central—comes to mind. The idea is that creation comes first, commentary afterwards. Eden, then Babel. The Torah, then the Talmud. The movie, then the review.

Chronologically speaking, this is not wrong. From an evolutionary or broadly historical perspective, it seems intuitively right that the creation of the universe precedes the emergence of language, which itself probably precedes the genesis of "art" as such, which surely precedes the development of any robust discourse of interpretation or criticism.

From a more mystical or theological point of view, however, it's unnecessary to view creation, language, art, and criticism as sequential, especially if we assume that meaning is purposefully infused into creation, woven into the fabric of the universe, that *logos* is always already present. *It all has to do with it*, as John Coltrane wrote.

[Permit, if you will, a mostly relevant digression: It's a mistake, I think, that we make when we assume that *logos* simply means "word," and this leads to some careless analogies. *Logos* is not so much about words—phonological, linguistic semantic units—as we know them, but about an ultimate reality. This reality can be difficult to name. For some, it simply refers to reason. For Christians, it is Christ himself. Chinese bibles translate *logos* as *dao*, the Way. However we define *logos*, it is clear there is more to meaning than mere words—sound, gesture, image, movement, and many other channels exist through which we understand and interpret the world and each other. That we can do so is a testament to something I would say is divine, a God-breathed consciousness, a spark of meaning and purpose, in us.]

What I want to suggest, then, is that the fact that we can make meaning at all should be seen as being of a piece with our participation in the created order, an intended side effect of our being something a little lower than the angels, as it were, who can know and mean. Even when we're knowing and meaning about rock and roll.

There are some thorny questions about meaning—specifically relating to music, language, and interpretation—when it comes to looking into why we bother to write about music at all. Thankfully, other writers have begun to delve into these questions, and in this chapter I talk about three works by other writers that do this well. For Carl Wilson in *Let's Talk About Love*, the question is why so many people love music by an artist he can't stand (music + interpretation). For Devon Powers in *Writing the Record*, the question is how the idea of rock criticism emerged in the 1960s when a group of writers for the *Village Voice* began asking how they could develop a new language for talking about music (language + music). For Ethan Hayden in *Sigur Rós's ( )*, the question is how an invented language, emptied of semantic content, can work in tandem with the semiotics of music, and somehow be made to mean (language + music + interpretation). All of these writers (one a music critic, one a scholar, one a composer) ask questions about listening to, loving, understanding, and writing about music, questions that suggest a larger, looming question about the very possibility of meaning.

***

Carl Wilson's *Let's Talk about Love* is the most feted book in Bloomsbury Academic's 33 1/3 series. The series comprises short books in various genres about classic pop albums, including everything from the Smiths' *Meat is Murder* to Nirvana's *In Utero* to the soundtrack to the Super Mario Brothers Nintendo game. These are books by and for what are usually called "music nerds," which is why Wilson's book came as a shock: its theme is the Céline Dion album *Let's Talk about Love*, the one that includes the theme from the movie *Titanic*, "My Heart Will Go On." This is not, strictly speaking, a music nerd's album; Céline Dion makes the kind of overwrought, populist schmaltz that readers and writers of the 33 1/3 series are predisposed to hate.

This, then, is Wilson's genius: rather than undertaking a critical dissection of the album itself, or an academic study of its significance, Wilson makes an earnest inquiry into why so many people love Céline Dion, and why he can't. The book's original sub-title was *A Journey to the End of Taste*, while the expanded edition, issued by Bloomsbury Academic in 2014, goes with the more on-the-nose *Why Other People Have Such Bad Taste*. Wilson makes few apologies about hating Céline Dion, but his investigation into why others love her is refreshingly open.

Wilson looks into various aspects of Dion's character that give her grassroots global appeal: being a non-American (she's French-Canadian), having a working-class Catholic upbringing in a large family and a beat-the-odds success story, singing vague love songs that are accessible to non-native English speakers, and so on. He leans heavily on the notion advanced by the French sociolo-gist Pierre Bourdieu that aesthetic taste, far from being driven by objective judgment or even a personal encounter with beauty, is, Wilson explains, "an array of symbolic associations we use to set ourselves apart from those whose social ranking is beneath us, and to take aim at the status we think we deserve."[4]

While he does not wholly agree with Bourdieu, Wilson ac-knowledges that his own musical prejudices are not simply aes-thetic; the social world a music critic like Wilson lives in—the hip, youngish, left-leaning political world of a Canadian urbanite who writes for *Slate* and the *New York Times*—constrains what he is able to love, and how he is able to interpret the language of an artist like Dion whose work is embraced by subcultures he isn't a part of: immigrants, drag queens, rural radio listeners.

4. Wilson, *Let's Talk about Love*, 90–91.

Interestingly, against this sociological backdrop, Wilson's explication of others' love for Céline Dion starts to sound something like faith, with Wilson as the kind of nonbeliever who looks at religion with admiration and even longing, but finds the whole enterprise intellectually disingenuous. He explicitly addresses this when he writes about cultural elites' distrust of sentimentality and melodrama, wondering if he has it wrong. Wilson admires John Cage's famous silent piece, *4'33,"* for its sangfroid, its anti-sentimentality: "Like Cage's silence, God's love is unspeakable, implacable, its gaze matter-of-fact. But human love is something else: We love in excess of God's love if we love at all. We love by heaping meaning on objective fact. If I believed in God, I might imagine this is what He created humans for, to give things more tenderness than He granted them."[5] (Wilson here is echoing J. D. Salinger in *Raise High the Roofbeam, Carpenters*, who was himself quoting R. H. Blyth, a scholar of literature and Zen Buddhism.) Wilson begins to wonder if it isn't truly human to exaggerate, to pile on the schmaltz until it becomes unbearable; "God or no God, it's hubris to pretend to know the correct amount of tenderness it is ours to grant," he concludes.[6]

Taste—which appears to be nothing more than love, in the end—seems to be something elusively subjective, even though it may be heavily influenced by social factors. Ultimately, *Let's Talk about Love* is a book about *caring* about music, a kind of deeper love that goes beyond liking or disliking particular genres or artists. This is underscored by the handful of response essays solicited for the book's expanded edition; most of the contributors write more about what they love (the band Television, Diana Ross, family members, disco dances) than respond directly to Wilson's original book. This, perhaps, is as it should be; writing about something you care about should beget others writing about what they care about, rather than nitpicky critiques-of-critiques. George Steiner would be pleased.

5. Wilson, *Let's Talk about Love*, 124–25.
6. Wilson, *Let's Talk about Love*, 125.

If *Let's Talk about Love* is a book that deals with *caring, Writing the Record* is one that deals with *mattering*, looking into how and why pop music, and writing about music, matter to people. When serious writing about popular music was in its infancy, everything was an open question: is rock and roll about art or business? Are newspaper columns about rock true criticism or ephemeral fluff? Should rock critics write mostly about music, or culture, or politics? Powers's book, adapted from her doctoral thesis, describes how the *Village Voice*, a venerable institution in the alt-weekly newspaper business until it unceremoniously went out of business in 2018, began to incorporate writing about rock music into its pages—completely separate, notably, from its sections on classical music and jazz—and how a handful of the *Voice* writers came to create what we now think of as rock criticism.

What seemed to matter most to these writers, in Powers's analysis, is the idea that as part of the rock and roll effort (remember that Meltzer quote), they were part of a new, vital movement, one that was as much cultural and political as it was artistic, which would bring about social change during the tumultuous 1960s. Powers draws on cultural theorists and on historical documents from the *Voice* and other publications, tracing the development of pop music as an important cultural force, the reckoning of "serious" critics with populist art forms when they could no longer be ignored, and the eventual development of pop criticism in the work of Richard Goldstein and Robert Christgau. These writers, and other public intellectuals of their generation (like Pauline Kael and Susan Sontag), were in large part responsible for making "low" forms of art the subject of serious thought and criticism.

From its earliest days, Powers shows, rock criticism was conflicted about what the purpose of rock and folk music—and writing about it—actually was. Rock seemed to carry with it some of the politics of the folk movement—the emphasis on authenticity, community, and grassroots politics—but by 1966, Goldstein was already lamenting the butchering of rock music by "public relations men, disc jockeys, emcees, executives, socko boffo copy boys, fabulous blondes, prophets, frauds, fakes"[7] and others involved in what Powers identifies as "hype"—the appropriation of underground music by mass media for commercial purposes.[8] By 1970, the idea of rock music as a unified social movement was dead, and the *Voice* critics lamented its fragmentation and commercialization. Even as they continued to write about rock music with, Powers writes, the "assumption that rock music listening should be a revolutionary experience politically, personally, emotionally, and intellectually," critics used their platforms to proclaim that rock was dead.[9]

The absence of the word "spiritually" from Powers's list, incidentally, should not be taken to mean that there is not a great deal of faith in the act of writing about music, even for the *Village Voice*. Many of the early rock critics seem to have been animated by a kind of utopian impulse, a longing for a left-wing eschaton, and seem to have been disappointed by its tarrying; nevertheless, they continued to document rock music and culture. It is perhaps worth noting that many of the early critics at the *Voice* were Jewish: Goldstein, Kael, and Ellen Willis. I am reminded of what the contemporary rock critic Douglas Wolk once told me, about working at his college radio station. A common practice was to put a plain white sticker on a record and write something about it. People would add other comments and eventually "have these long, almost Talmudic conversations," he said, about rock albums. The lesson Wolk learned: if you were serious about music, you wrote about it. This sort of commentary, I think, is part of the impulse I described earlier: the desire to know, to understand, to make meaning about something you hold dear.

While Powers's analysis tends to focus on the macro- and micro-politics the *Voice* writers were embedded in, her final chapter, "Mattering," gets at something deeper. While Robert Christgau gave his album-review column the only partly tongue-in-cheek title "Consumer Guide," he also referred to the essential core of

---

7. Goldstein, "Giraffe Hunters," quoted in Powers, *Writing the Record*, 74.

8. Powers, *Writing the Record*, 75.

9. Powers, *Writing the Record*, 97

rock writing as "The Mattering."[10] It is clear that music has an enormous amount of influence in people's lives, socially, culturally, and even spiritually; religious music is the most obvious genre to fit that bill, but as the theologian Jeffrey F. Keuss argues in his book *Your Neighbor's Hymnal*, popular music, too, fills an almost liturgical need in many peoples' lives. Powers concludes her chapter definitively: "the ability to listen, write, and read together—with music as our muse, our riddle, our antagonist—deserves unwavering faith and resolute defense."[11] This is in part, she argues, because cultural vitality is at stake. Perhaps on an altogether higher level, our very sense of who we are and why *anything* matters is at stake.

Ethan Hayden's book, *Sigur Rós's ( )*, about the album of the same name (well, "name") by the Icelandic band Sigur Rós, though the shortest of those discussed here, is the most dense. Drawing on a variety of scholarly sources on music, language, and semiotics, Hayden attempts to parse the band's ethereal third album, which is sung entirely in a made-up language known as *Vonlenska*, or Hopelandic (mostly short syllables like *yu, fy, sy, lo,* and *so*). It is a book about, among other things, "filling in gaps, about interpreting things we can't possibly understand, but feel very deeply that we do," and about "language, about languages we don't understand, about languages that aren't meant to be understood," Hayden writes.[12]

Sigur Rós is one of the most prominent post-rock bands of the last decade, using rock instrumentation to create music that is at times more neoclassical than pop. The band's aesthetic is redolent with grandeur and awe: songs slowly build, over the course of five to ten minutes, from minimalist riffs to triumphant crescendos. Their influence can be seen in contemporary rock music—even a pop band like Coldplay owes something to Sigur Rós—and in contemporary evangelical religious music (a number of Christian post-rock bands I interviewed for an article some years ago described Sigur Rós as both a musical and spiritual influence—more

10. Powers, *Writing the Record*, 124.

11. Powers, *Writing the Record*, 136.

12. Hayden, *Sigur Rós's ( )*, 3 and 4.

about this later). One of the hallmarks of their sound is Jón Þór "Jónsi" Birgisson's otherworldly falsetto, which often functions more like an instrument than a voice.

Hayden explores what it means for ( ) to be an album intentionally devoid of linguistic meaning which many listeners nevertheless experience as meaningful. The book's four main chapters, "Nonsense," "Voice," "Space," and "Hope" deal with different aspects of the album's sounds and what they mean. He describes a variety of invented languages, from xenoglossia (alien language) to echolalia (imitations of language) to glossolalia (speaking in tongues), noting that languages that lack an inherent semantic structure, like Sigur Rós's Hopelandic, paradoxically mean nothing but *can* mean anything; the listener is invited to fill in the gaps. Hayden argues that Hopelandic "actively resists signification," thus relying primarily on the sound of Jónsi's voice to make it what it is.[13]

What *is* it, exactly? Why do so many people seem moved by a meaningless language? In his introduction, Hayden claims that he does not intend to interpret the album, and in fact concludes the book by suggesting that the music has "no real reason at all" and that he would rather "let nothingness be nothingness" than encourage "people solipsistically meditating on their own individual meanings."[14]

I understand what he means—again, preferring the creation to the commentary—but the cat is already out of the bag when you manage to write, as Hayden did, 144 pages about this nothingness. And as Hayden would admit, Sigur Rós's music is not nothing. Regardless of its alleged semantic emptiness, it's still this primary act of creation, this making, that prods a critic to take notes on what he or she sees or hears, to explain it to others. By writing about even "nonsensical" music, a critic takes part in the construction of meaning—a meaning which doesn't even have to be semantic, by the way; Hayden uses Julia Kristeva's distinction between the symbolic (language) and the semiotic (the expression of "instinctual

13. Hayden, *Sigur Rós's ( )*, 55.
14. Hayden, *Sigur Rós's ( )*, 7 and 144.

drives") to suggest that there are meanings somehow before, or beyond, or beneath language.[15] Perhaps it's fitting, then, that Hayden doesn't present his work as a definitive statement of what the album is "about." Don't many of us intuit a sort of *ur*-meaning beyond our own semiotic capabilities, assuming our attempts to speak or sing or write fall short of a more perfect expression of something we can't quite name? Might that not be the mystery that a "meaningless" musical language embraces?

***

Language may, of course, be the best tool we have to try to get at the ineffable qualities Hayden investigates about nonsense—and Wilson about love, and Powers about criticism—or indeed to get at any understanding of ourselves and our universe, which is why so many books have been written not only about music, but about all kinds of human symbolic behavior.

Perhaps it is like this: the ground we see before us is covered in pristine snow. To make anything, to make music or art or literature or a sound or a gesture, is to make a mark in the snow. To react and interpret, to say something about what you've seen, is to make more tracks. They begin to blur together in a kind of conversation. We're all going somewhere, following each other, or making our own paths.

The metaphor is overwrought, I'm afraid, but this is the central question about meaning: Why is there snow—the raw materials for meaning-making, I mean—at all? What abstruse purpose does the force that sustains the universe have in making us, as the rhetorician Kenneth Burke claimed, a "symbol-using (symbol-making, symbol-misusing) animal"?[16] It seems to me that we come from meaning, we are made from meaning, and we are desperate or doomed or determined to continue to make and remake it from the materials we've been given—our voices, our hands, our

---

15. Hayden, *Sigur Rós's ( )*, 65.
16. Burke, *Language as Symbolic Action*, 16.

minds—and the technologies we've made, among which writing has been paramount for almost all of our history.

The books I've mentioned here are fascinating volumes about (in part) what it means to write about music, but more than that, they are underwritten by the belief that it is somehow a worthwhile endeavor to make meaning out of meaning. This itself, as George Steiner argues in *Real Presences*, is "a wager on transcendence," or "a wager on a relationship . . . between word and world . . . precisely bounded by that which reinsures it."[17] We write about music, or about art, or about writing, because we seem, in the end, to have faith that all this meaning does, well, *mean* something.

17. Steiner, *Real Presences*, 214 and 216.

(I Feel Sad That Chris Walla Is No Longer in Death Cab for Cutie and Other Emotions)

I miss you already
I haven't seen Death Cab live since probably about 2007
But have you seen who they got to replace you
There is a guy with a big beard playing the keyboard
and also a very dapper-looking guy in a plaid shirt from Portland
*   playing the guitar*
they had to get two dudes to replace you
that is how good you are
Also I don't know if the other guitar dude also plays a bass
on "We Looked Like Giants" like you did but even if he does
I am sure he doesn't do it the way you did
Also can we briefly talk about what I like to call the
"Death Cab Leg Dance"
(Actually that's not true I sometimes call it the "Ben Gibbard Leg
*   Dance"*
and sometimes the "Chris Walla Leg Dance" and really it is probably
*   just the awkward leg wiggle that most white indie rock dudes*
do when they want to show how much they are enjoying the music but
*   are unable to actually do a dance)*
Anyway it was always pretty fun watching the two of you guys do that
when things really got going, like on "We Laugh Indoors"
so I'm sad we don't get to see that anymore,
Although like I said I haven't been to a show in years and frankly I
*   barely go to rock shows at all anymore because I am a university*
*   professor with kids now*

Also to be honest I always sort of thought you were what would
traditionally be called the "lead guitarist" but someone pointed out
to me that Ben Gibbard actually plays a lot of the memorable riffs
that I like
However
This actually makes me miss you even more because you were sort
of both the lead guitarist and both the rhythm guitarist and it
was so badass when you'd eventually both play the same riff in
unison—here I am particularly thinking of the bridge of "You Are
a Tourist"
I digress, because this is supposed to be about how I miss you
And in an intangible way I do sort of, even though I only met you once
At a coffee shop in Seattle in maybe 2003 when I interviewed you for a
magazine
and you told me never to accept a free electric organ if offered one
(which advice I can honestly say I have followed)
And I feel strange about this intangible way in which I miss you
because
it forces me to confront a lot of things I would rather not, such as:

why am I still a "fan" of rock bands even though I am forty years old
and
why do I feel compelled to write in a semi-personal way about people I
have met either never or only once fifteen years ago
and
why have I funneled a lot of the emotional content of my life through
songs other people wrote and played
and
why do I even bother to feel embarrassed about this when it is probably
a really normal way to feel
and so on.

Anyway you are super good at the guitar and
I'll always appreciate the transcendent way you were able to
articulate longing and sadness with very few notes on songs like
"Transatlanticism"
and if I ever do go see Death Cab again I will enjoy that song
But somehow not in the same way I would have

What Dancing about Architecture Does, or How Words and Dreams and a Million Screams Make Weezer

If I speak in the tongues of men and of angels, but have not love, I am a noisy gong or a clanging cymbal.

—St. Paul, 1 Corinthians 13:1

CLANG CLANG CLANG CLANG

—The bell of Patrick Wilson's ride cymbal
at the beginning of "Tired of Sex"

Let's start with the clanging.

Wilson's clanging is more than a count into the song: it's the Big Bang, the beginning of an attempt to shepherd the chaos of electrical noise into a rhythmic structure. Most of us remember the four hits on the bell of Wilson's ride cymbal as the beginning of *Pinkerton*, but we forget the record actually begins with a squall of guitar feedback.

The whole record follows after the clanging. *Pinkerton* is a record about a guy who, to paraphrase St. Paul, pretty much definitely "has not love." If you've got it (love, bliss, enlightenment) you don't make a rock record about it. You don't even need to talk about it. You just *be* in it. But if you are filled with and plagued by desire, if you are straining for something that eludes you, you talk about it, and make a record of your heart.

So there is the clanging, banging, buzzing record—which, as Rivers Cuomo sings on "El Scorcho," he made because he *couldn't* talk about what it was he wanted to talk about. And now, paradoxically, for twenty-five years, we have been talking—and writing—about it. There is the making of something, and then there is the interpretation of it, and the problem, writes George Steiner, is that "aesthetic perception knows no Archimedean point outside discourse. The root of all talk is talk."[1] Once the first move has been made, everything else is commentary. The Russian literary critic M. M. Bakhtin put it this way: "any speaker is himself a respondent to a greater or lesser degree. He is not, after all, the first speaker, the one who disturbs the eternal silence of the universe."[2]

Say, then, that *Pinkerton* is the act of creation that has disturbed the eternal silence. What comes next is commentary upon commentary upon commentary, until by the time someone like me is writing about *Pinkerton* in 2021, I'm not writing about *Pinkerton* anymore; I'm writing about twenty-five years of people writing about Weezer after *Pinkerton*. What's significant about this is that by doing this, I'm helping to make Weezer and *Pinkerton* what they are to me, and to you, and even to the band.

I love *Pinkerton* for the raw material it is made of, of course: the off-mic screams (especially the "YEAAHHHH!" before the final chorus of "Getchoo"), the classical, almost baroque sensibilities of the bridges and solos, the honest weirdness of the lyrics, the buzz and dirtiness of it, and the way it sounds exactly like what being a nineteen-to-twenty-five-year-old white American dude in the nineties feels like. It's a beautiful record. That's important. But it's not *too* important.

See, there are two significant things about how we experience records. First: yes, what I love about *Pinkerton* has a lot to do with how it felt to first hear it, to play it into my life, the way it inhabited me and I inhabited it when I was eighteen. But second, there's the

1. Steiner, *Real Presences*, 61.
2. Bakhtin, "Problem of Speech Genres," 69.

way that the other Catholic school kids I was playing in a band with at the time (the ones who introduced me to Weezer because they wanted to cover "Say It Ain't So") told me not to bother buying it. The Blue Album was way better, they said. The songs were better; the guitar solos were better. *Pinkerton* was weird and bad, they said. *More like Rivers Homo*, they said. Too many feelings, too little shredding.

They were wrong, but what they said mattered, just like it mattered when Cuomo himself disowned *Pinkerton* in print, and when *Rolling Stone* revised their 1996 three-star review of *Pinkerton* to five stars in 2004, and when Cuomo said that he loved *Pinkerton* again in an interview a few years ago. The music matters, but the interpretation, the reaction, the writing, the commentary matters, too. Maybe even more.

The story of *Pinkerton*, as it turns out, is a story that stretches well beyond the period the album was made and released. It's a story of how the discourse universe surrounding Weezer was thrown into turmoil because nobody could agree on how good or bad or important the album was. It's the story of a band and its fans starting out on the same rhetorical team, and then breaking up, and then slowly coming back together, all through the textual world of "music writing."

The boundaries between (a) professional critic, (b) amateur appreciator, and (c) dude in a rock band are blurry in this world. We share a vocabulary, a love of the stuff of rock and roll, a discourse universe. All three of these overlapping communities are equally important in making music mean what it means, and we're often members of one or more or all of them at the same time. We are all, those of us in the fan/critic/artist orbit, the ones making all popular music mean what it means, and we do this in large part by writing about it.

Especially in an age where more texts are being produced than ever, we are all "music writers." You don't have to look very far for examples of this. Take Operation Space Opera, a group of Weezer fans who so loved Weezer's unreleased 1995 album *Songs from the Black Hole*—and so hated what Weezer had become since then—that they formed a band and rerecorded the entire album, releasing it online in 2012. They call Rivers Cuomo a "gormless dunce" in the liner notes,[3] but they lovingly, painstakingly record his songs, excavating them, saving them so others will hear. Fans, critics, band, all in one record. This is the kind of discourse those of us in the pop music universe produce all the time.

"Discourse," to the people who analyze it for a living, is not the jokey thing people complain about on social media—like "rhetoric" before it, "discourse" has become a word that means "people talking about politics in a really obnoxious way" in popular culture. For academics, though, it means basically the same thing as talk—"talk" here meaning language-in-use, anything beyond the word or sentence, which includes writing. For traditional linguists, discourse is just language in context. It's studying how people communicate instead of just studying how verbs are conjugated. Discourse is pretty much all human symbolic behavior, which is pretty much all human behavior, and it actually creates the world we live in.

The whole human cultural universe is a fragile enterprise constructed by language, so if you want to study anything about human culture, like, say, why a lot of people think *Pinkerton* is a great record and wish for more albums to be made that sound like it, and why they write about how much they hate Weezer albums that are not *Pinkerton*, discourse analysis is a good place to start. The tools of discourse analysis aren't so different from the ones that would be used by anyone carefully studying any other text. The difference is that instead of studying Shakespeare, we're studying a whole host of texts that have been written about *Pinkerton*.

Linguists have tended to ignore popular music, because they see its language as somehow "inauthentic," and even discourse and writing scholars have not seriously delved into the world of pop music writing. *Pinkerton*, though, seems like a great place to start. Charles Bazerman and Paul Prior define the discipline of writing studies as one that examines "what writing does and how it does

---

3. Operation Space Opera, *Songs from the Black Hole* (liner notes).

it."[4] What music writing does, really, is construct meaning: it actually makes the important things we know and love about bands and albums and even ourselves. *Pinkerton* is a great example.

Although Weezer fans are accustomed to splitting the band's history into pre- and post-*Pinkerton* periods, it's important to remember that *Pinkerton* itself was seen as a shocking departure from *Weezer*, their well-regarded debut also known as the Blue Album. We forget how Weezer was received in the music press when the band started—not as emo pioneers or even the standard-bearers of "geek rock" they are now (Rivers Cuomo didn't even wear glasses in the album art for the first two records!)—their first mention in a 1994 *Billboard* article describes the band as "tart punk-popsters,"[5] which seems odd, now—and how critics and others reacted to *Pinkerton* upon its release. Eventually, writing about Weezer started to contribute to the band's "geek rock" image and by the time the band emerged for its 2001 comeback, Cuomo was never seen without his black Ray-Bans.

Weezer was also, from the beginning, involved in amateur/fan music writing (the band and its fan club collaboratively produced the *Weezine*, which was mailed to members) and the then-burgeoning web culture, when the band's fanbase started to coalesce around *Pinkerton*. Weezer and Rivers Cuomo were clearly interested in communicating through writing, including the "Karl's Corner" section of Weezer's website (written by the band's longtime roadie, "fifth member," and documentarian, Karl Koch), articles Cuomo wrote for magazines, and the highly intertextual liner notes to *Pinkerton*, which include references to Puccini, Camille Paglia, comic book artist Joe Matt, and guitarist Yngwie Malmsteen, among others.

It wasn't until after Weezer's post-*Pinkerton* hiatus that it became clear what an important album *Pinkerton* was; the way we found out was via reviews like the one Spencer Owen wrote for Pitchfork in May 2001, the most memorable excerpt of which reads "No! Weezer! NO!! Where has Rivers Cuomo gone? What

4. Bazerman and Prior, introduction to *What Writing Does*, 6.

5. Morris, "Geffen's Modern Rock Methodology," 124.

has he done? What has happened to Weezer?! WHERE ARE THE REAL WEEZER?!!"[6]

Owen's desperate pleas were echoed by critics and fans. The idea of *Pinkerton* as Weezer's best album emerged as a side effect of fan/critic reactions to its follow-up, the Green Album. It's interesting to see how Cuomo was portrayed in the media during this period: as a cold, unemotional songwriting machine. In fact, it was the notion that the Green Album and *Maladroit* were "unemotional" that further cemented the idea that *Pinkerton* was an emo masterpiece. (This period also gave rise to the Matt Sharp Made Weezer Good theory, with a number of writers positing that Matt Sharp's ineffable contributions to the band and to *Pinkerton* in particular were the band's true heart and soul.)

While the Weezer discourse universe was heaping acclaim on *Pinkerton*, Cuomo was publicly denouncing the album as "sick" and calling his fans "little bitches"; thus began a kind of rhetorical antagonism between the band and fans/critics that would last for years, largely based on disagreements about *Pinkerton*. Cuomo's prickly discursive relations with fans can be seen in texts from this period, including the "Rivers Correspondence Board" message board, in which Cuomo interacted with fans (memorably referring to the song "Only in Dreams" with the neologistic portmanteau "DISNEYGAY"), lyrics from *Maladroit* (many of which address the band's frosty relationship with its audience), and the blog of Cuomo's personal assistant Sheeny Bang, which depicted Cuomo's awkwardness and resentment around his fans.

The release of *Make Believe* in 2005 saw a ramp-up of discursive antagonism toward Weezer, again largely based on their having again made an album that didn't sound like *Pinkerton*. Pitchfork's gleefully negative review (0.4/10) questioned whether the album retroactively tarnished the legacy of Weezer's early albums, and in particular whether *Pinkerton* was in fact as bad as *Make Believe*.[7] Interestingly, though, the album was an enormous commercial success, selling nearly four million copies worldwide.

6. Owen, review of *Weezer (Green Album)*.

7. Mitchum, review of *Make Believe*.

Weezer-related discourse around this time suggests the emergence of a kind of split between "original" or "true" fans of the band, who wrote about being disappointed and angry with the band with each new release, and newer fans who were introduced to the group via singles like "Beverly Hills" or "Pork and Beans." (To say nothing of the mainstream music press, which tended to give Weezer records favorable if tepid reviews during this period.) While this mostly played out along age-related lines, it was also a matter of identification: to proclaim, boldly, on the internet, your *hatred* for Weezer (regardless of how old you were in 1996) was in some sense to *love* the "real Weezer" who made *Pinkerton*.

This period also coincided with the rise of blogging and social media, which perhaps lessened the impact of professional music writing and increased that of amateur reviews and/or "takes." As always, *Pinkerton* remained at the center of the debate about the band. In recent years (especially since 2014), perhaps surprisingly, there has been a kind of discursive *rapprochement* reached by Weezer and its fans (and critics), during a period in which, as Ryan McNutt wrote for *Chart Attack*, "for once, [Cuomo is] thinking of his audience, thinking of what *I* might like."[8] The band and Cuomo began more intentionally drawing on their older material after the release of *Hurley*, and this culminated in the band and its fans getting rhetorically (and physically) closer: the Weezer Cruise (during which Cuomo read selections from his *Pinkerton*-era diary), the Memories tour(s) (in which the band played the Blue Album and *Pinkerton* from beginning to end) and the release of *Everything Will Be Alright in the End*, the band's first album in years to be well-received by fans. These positive vibes were not (only) musical, but rhetorical; the band appeared to align itself with the criticisms raised by its "real" and "true" fans in the album's promotional materials, interviews, marketing campaign, and even lyrics, which include an actual apology (Sorry guys / I didn't realize that I needed you so much") for decisions the band had been making for years.

8. McNutt, "Back to the Shack."

This period also saw the release of *The Pinkerton Diaries*, the deluxe reissue of *Pinkerton*, and Cuomo's own public reassessment of the album ("I think it's a brilliant album; I love it," he told *Exclaim!* in 2011).[9] While this could be read as a cynical attempt to capitalize on fans' desires, or Cuomo's own coming to terms with his past, really, the band's newfound embrace of *Pinkerton* was Weezer's return to the same discursive "team" as its fans, making irenic rhetorical moves to reunite a fractured fan/critic/artist community. (It's no accident that the band's charmingly anachronistic "fan club" started up again for the first time in years, complete with mailed welcome letters.)

In the end, the story of *Pinkerton* is a story of a band and its fans starting out together, growing apart, and eventually reuniting—all through various forms of what have come to be known as "music writing." Why are Weezer fans so invested in *Pinkerton* and in the band itself? For a band that has made so many unpopular moves, its fans (myself included) seem remarkably unwilling to give them up. Ultimately, it seems that talking shit about Weezer and *Pinkerton* has to do with *loving* the band and the album, and that writing about music, even critical and snarky and angry writing about music, is an enterprise people engage in because we deeply care about music, and about culture, and even, in the end, about each other.

What is "music writing," though, really? It's no longer (if it ever was) just Robert Christgau's column, or the reviews section of *Rolling Stone*, or whatever Pitchfork posts. Blogs, websites, tweets, pamphlets, Facebook, vlogs, message boards: it's all music writing. It's all musical discourse.

Musical discourse is its own discourse universe. The orbits of fan/critic/artist, and the writing they produce, is so tangled up in the unique enterprise of making, sustaining, and loving popular music, that it's necessary to approach it on its own terms. The Russian scholar Evgeniya Aleshinskaya made a foray into this realm a few years ago with her article "Key Components of Musical Discourse Analysis" which looks at discourse about pop music

9. Cuomo, quoted in Gormely, "Rivers Runs Through It."

as "representing specific aspects of the social (musical) sphere."[10] She rightly sees that musical discourse, in some important ways, sustains what is almost a way of life for many of us. Those of us who live in a universe where pop music is important—who feel our lives are tightly bound up with, driven by, lived *to* music—recognize that musical discourse, music writing, needs to be looked at by people who understand it from the inside. (Much more of this in the next chapter.)

Chuck Klosterman wrote, in *Eating the Dinosaur*: "People are generally disappointed by Weezer albums."[11] It's hard to put it more succinctly than that. It is the central fact of most Weezer fans' fandom. What people write about when they write about Weezer, usually, is why they are angry at Weezer for having made an album that is not *Pinkerton*. Like anyone else who loved Weezer before the twenty-first century, it is difficult for me to stop caring about them, even though they keep making records I mostly do not love. Academic questions about the meaning of Weezer-related discourse aside, I really do believe—whether I'm right or not, whether it's fair or not—that *Pinkerton* is just ineffably way, way, *way* better than anything they've done since. The album is shot through with what I take to be energy, passion, desire, and anguish in ways that astonish me every time I listen. The point is, though, that there's no way for us to know whether we'd like *Make Believe* or *Hurley* without *Pinkerton*. And frankly, there couldn't *be* a *Make Believe* or *Hurley* without *Pinkerton*. Once the act of creation has occurred, every subsequent utterance—linguistic, or musical, or both—is in some way a speaking/writing back.

You may have noticed this is starting to feel like circles within circles: for several thousand words, I've been writing about Weezer and *Pinkerton* by writing about people writing about Weezer and *Pinkerton*. You are, in fact, reading writing about writing about music. Is this even a thing? Is there anything *there*? I think there is: the weight and heft, the buzz and crash and wounded screams of *Pinkerton*. If there weren't something deeply compelling and

10. Aleshinskaya, "Musical Discourse Analysis," 423.

11. Klosterman, *Eating the Dinosaur*, 193.

unusual about how well-written and well-made *Pinkerton* is, there would be no reason for writers and fans and even the band itself to talk and write about it every time Weezer does something.

And the very idea of discourse doesn't mean there isn't any substance to the world—it's just that the *there* is *everywhere*, that we're all much more implicated in what *is* there than we might have believed. We make *Pinkerton* what it is by talking about it, writing about it, and caring about it. If it's worth writing about music (and it is), then it's worth writing about writing about music, because writing plays such a huge part in making music what it is and what it means. That's why we keep doing it: because this stuff matters. And because even if you speak with the tongues of men and angels, if you love anything this much, you've got to make a record of it.

(A List of Things That Might Happen
When You Write about Music)

*You might be desperate for money and put ads up on Craigslist
offering to write band bios for twenty-five dollars. You might get a
few clients but never do the work because their music is so awful
that you feel bad for them and for yourself.*

*You might write a bio for your friend's band that somehow has
twenty million plays on Spotify and he might offer you fifty dollars
but you might turn him down because you knew him when he was
recording aimless twenty-minute ambient jams in his dorm room.*

*You might get an internet comment from the singer of your favorite
band. It might say "this is the most interesting review of our work
I have ever read." Fifteen years later you might ask that singer for
free tickets to their sold-out show at the Orpheum via Twitter and
he might say OK. A few months after that you might see that same
singer riding his bike in the rain when you are on your way to work.*

*You might get an email from a bass guitarist who is also an Ortho-
dox priest that includes the sentence "you get us."*

*You might take literally a message from a band's manager who says
"come hang out at the show." You might browbeat the opening band
into giving you a free copy of their new record because you tell them
you reviewed their first one for a national magazine and you might
spend an hour asking after the manager, trying to figure out how*

to get backstage, unsuccessfully. You might realize that he did not actually want you to hang out with the band. You might realize that you do not actually want to hang out with the band. You might rethink your priorities. You might stop going to rock shows for a while.

You might write a slightly too-personal essay that mentions a singer you love and might always wonder if he read it and whether he felt weird about it. You might wonder this about every band you ever write about.

You might write an essay about a weird experience you had with a band you liked when you were a teenager but that you don't listen to anymore. Two hundred people might comment on the article online, 85 percent of whom might tell you that you are a stupid idiot.

You might write an article about how a songwriter you like made you sad because of some songs he wrote. His fans might accuse you of being a closed-minded idiot on the internet. He might write something that makes you think he pretty much agrees with them. You might write his manager an email explaining that you feel you have something to apologize for, even if you might not really, but you just feel so bad you have to do something.

You might start to think the internet was altogether a bad idea.

You might be a twenty-seven-year-old writer with dozens of bylines and a graduate degree, interviewing a guy from a band you don't care about for an article you don't care about for a publication you don't care about and have a splitting headache because you hate your job, and ask him stupid questions. He might ask you if this is an article for a school newspaper.

You might start reading blogs by people you consider your peers. You might watch them go from being bloggers and stringers for weeklies to freelancers for Spin *and* Rolling Stone *to staff writers at*

Pitchfork *to managers of whole departments at Google and MTV and Apple. You might feel jealous of them as you sit down to grade thirty-six essays by first-year university students.*

You might ask Ben Gibbard a dumb question when you interview him.

You might try and fail to meet one of your favorite songwriters in Dallas, Texas.

You might write a satirical letter to the music editor of a weekly newspaper when you move to a new city hoping that he might notice you. He might indeed notice you and you might win a T-shirt and four tickets to concerts, which you might sell on Craigslist for a total of $250. He might make fun of you in print for several weeks and you might never write for his newspaper.

You might write three reviews for a weekly newspaper in Denver, Colorado for no money. They might not be printed.

You might write two reviews for a magazine in Chico, California for seven dollars apiece but you might not be paid.

You might write a feature for a national magazine and after you submit it the editor might not respond to your emails or phone calls for eight months, but he might eventually publish your article, with no explanation.

You might write a book about music and you might get emails from five or ten people who liked it, which might feel awesome. You might become legit friends with some of these people. You might discover, ten years later, that you have sold exactly 231 copies of this book, and this might feel like about the right amount.

Your wife might not ever read anything you write, which is totally fine.

You might write album reviews for no money for years.

You might make $3,000 a year from writing about music.

You might make zero dollars a year from writing about music.

You might get emails from people who are mad at you for not liking their favorite bands. This might make you sad and even scared and might be one of the reasons you stop writing album reviews.

You might tell everyone you've stopped writing about music but one afternoon feel restless and pitch an editor you know.

You might find yourself in Portland, Oregon, at Berbati's Pan. You might be almost shaking with nerves because earlier that day at a friend's wedding someone told you that a beautiful woman with a beautiful voice called your name from the stage of Seattle's Tractor Tavern last night, and said she would kiss you if you were in attendance, and you might see that woman sitting at a table after playing one of the most wonderful shows you've ever seen. Someone else might tell you her band read your blurb about their show on the radio that morning and said it was the nicest thing anyone had ever written about them. Your girlfriend might finally tell you to get over yourself and you might meet the songwriter and he might give you a hug. Some years later you might go to the Tractor Tavern and meet the woman and remind her about the time she said she'd kiss you and she'll say "I'm married" and you'll say "I am too" and then she might kiss you on the cheek right then and there, with your wife standing next to you.

You might stop writing about music for a long time.

You might always be the kind of person who writes about music.

31

How Dancing about Architecture Is Possible, or What is This, and Is It Any Good?

> I know it when I see it.
>
> —SUPREME COURT JUSTICE POTTER STEWART,
> ON THE DEFINITION OF PORNOGRAPHY, 1964

> My aesthetic point of evaluating something is basically the same as it was when I was twelve: it's like, "Does this rule?" . . . But the thing is, I get at that a lot of different ways.
>
> —ANDREW BEAUJON AT THE 2007
> *FESTIVAL OF FAITH AND MUSIC*

I once attended a concert by Chanticleer, a men's choral ensemble started in 1978 as a vehicle for performing classical choral music from the medieval and Renaissance periods. The program for the evening consisted of a variety of pieces from a wide range of historical periods, including works by well-known composers like Johannes Brahms, Eric Whitacre, and Karlheinz Stockhausen. None of the sections of this "classical" repertoire were labeled "classical"—they were merely listed by name and composer. The final section of the program, however, was labeled "Popular Songs." The implication was clear: the audience could expect a serious concert of classical music, and at the end, as a "fun" bonus, the group would perform some pop songs, such as George Gershwin's "Love Walked In" and Cole Porter's "It's All Right with Me." While

Gershwin and Porter, who wrote their music during the first half of the twentieth century, are not the artists whom the average person today might think of when the words "pop music" are mentioned, this purposeful separation of pop from other types of music remains persistent.

To use language is to categorize, to separate things from each other in order to better understand them, and, in so doing, ultimately to create a kind of reality. "Men seek for vocabularies that will be faithful *reflections* of reality," wrote Kenneth Burke in *A Grammar of Motives*. "To this end, they must develop vocabularies that are *selections* of reality. And any selection of reality must, in certain circumstances, function as a *deflection* of reality."[1] In other words, when humans use language to describe reality, we also limit it. In naming certain things art, for example, we name others not-art. Within art, we make further distinctions with language: we name abstract art, and so some art is non-abstract art. Impressionist art is not printmaking, sculpture is not poetry, modern dance is not ballet, and popular music is not classical music. When we separate types of artistic expression into categories, we imply that each possesses some characteristics that make it what it is.

Vocabularies of definition lead naturally into vocabularies of evaluation. Once we have decided defining characteristics—not always an easy task—we can begin to determine not only whether a particular piece conforms to them, but also whether some pieces fulfill them more fully, or "better," than others do. It becomes possible to determine, for example, whether something is a pop song and whether or not it is a good pop song. Together, then, the following two questions make up the most persistent questions about musical artifacts, which need to be considered before we decide whether and how it is possible to write about them:

1. What is this?

and

2. Is it any good?

1. Burke, *Grammar of Motives*, 59.

These questions assert themselves in the realm of popular music as much as anywhere else, and here I attempt not to wholly answer them, but to determine whether we can arrive at some criteria for *how* to answer them. The impetus here is both personal and professional: a desire to come to a better understanding of the aesthetics of popular music, and whether critics and fans of pop music (like myself) can work toward a sensible understanding of how to write about it in a "critical" way.

The ideas explored here are influenced by a number of fancy-pants theorists, most notably Theodor Adorno and Arthur Danto, but I don't claim to be an expert in this area. I am also trying to trust my instincts as someone immersed in the pop music world (or what I refer to here as the *popworld*) as a participant-observer. The main goal here is not simply to identify characteristics of popular music that make it separate from other understandings of art or music, or even whether popular music can be considered art by any criteria (that is another argument for those with stronger wills and more patience than I); rather, I attempt to identify some possible ways by which to understand definitions and evaluations of pop music. My conclusions are necessarily colored by my experience, and though I favor ideas of popular music as a form of expression defined by a combined social/aesthetic function and best evaluated by those people who are invested in pop music as a social/aesthetic community, the points outlined here should be understood as an exploration rather than a definitive argument.

In "Definitions of Popular Music: Recycled," Gaynor Jones and Jay Rahn point out that most definitions of popular music suffer from a "narrowness of vision" and a tendency toward "categorical statements" about whether music is or is not popular, when in fact the meaning of "popular music" has never remained fixed.[2] There are a few possible ways of defining popular music aesthetically: these include Adorno's definition of pop as being the opposite of "serious music";[3] an application of Danto's "artworld" theory to pop music; and a discussion of whether popular music

2. Jones and Rahn, "Definitions of Popular Music," 80.
3. Adorno, "On Popular Music," 17.

34

can be identified by characteristic musical traits. Is there a compelling reason that so many different musicians, from Metallica to Céline Dion to the Beatles, can be found in the same section in the inventory of a record store? Is there an overarching commonality linking Jay-Z to John Mayer? Many people, it seems, pop fans or not, are like Justice Stewart when it comes to pop music: we can't exactly define it, but we know it when we see it.

Many critics and philosophers use the term "rock" when referring to popular music, but this word presents two difficulties. First, although rock is ostensibly a shortening of "rock and roll," a genre which emerged in the 1950s, lately it has come to connote a specific vein of rock and roll involving distorted guitars and aggressive vocals—a style typified by the 1970s group Led Zeppelin. Richard Meltzer (*The Aesthetics of Rock*) and Theodore Gracyk (*Rhythm and Noise: An Aesthetics of Rock*) have both written volumes bearing the words "aesthetics of rock," but their examples include artists from Elvis Costello to the Shangri-La's to Sonny and Cher, who can hardly be called purveyors of "rock" music by this definition. Second, even "rock" meaning "rock and roll" excludes a number of similar musics. Reebee Garofalo cites rock and roll's defining characteristics as "its urban orientation, focus on youth culture, and appeal to working-class sensibilities, and its relationship to technology and African American musical influences and performance styles."[4] These characteristics, however, are equally applicable to a number of other contemporary music genres, such as rap and "dance" or electronic music, however. The *New York Times* pop music critic Kelefa Sanneh understands the limitations of rock as a category, and calls this bias toward rock "rockism," or a prejudice against pop music that does not conform to "the rock rules of the 1970s."[5] Therefore, it seems that an appellation like "pop," because it does not limit us to a particular sub-genre of music the way "rock" can, is preferable. But "pop" raises its own questions.

4. Garofalo, *Rockin' Out*, 4.
5. Sanneh, "Rap Against Rockism."

"Pop" is, of course, short for "popular," but if pop music is determined by actual popularity in terms of record sales and size of fan bases, then Megadeth (a "pop" metal band) and the Spice Girls (a dance-pop group) belong in the same aesthetic category, but anyone with ears to hear knows that they do not sound even remotely alike, although both groups employ rhythm, melody, lyrics, verses and choruses, and the like. Additionally, pop connotes music primarily created for entertainment or diversion, something altogether "lighter" than what Adorno calls "serious music." If pop music is somehow non-serious, however, what of bands who craft music with utter reverence and an almost classical gravitas, like Radiohead? If Megadeth should not be categorized with the Spice Girls for reasons of musical dissimilarity, Radiohead does not belong with Megadeth for reasons of seriousness. Then again, even Radiohead *have* written un-serious pop songs: Christopher O'Riley, a classical pianist who has adapted the works of Radiohead for piano, will not adapt their international pop hit "Creep," suggesting that doing so "might really step over the line into a Muzak version."[6] Radiohead themselves have dismissed the song as overly simplistic, at one time refusing to play the song live for years. Radiohead's singer Thom Yorke describes "Creep" as inconsequential and trite, famously comparing it to other popular "alternative" pop songs of the 1990s as being "fridge buzz": "when you're driving around and around, and you have the alternative stations on in the background, or in your hotel room, it's just like a fridge buzzing."[7] So "pop" maybe is preferable to "rock," but using the term seems to do little more than remove musical restrictions from the definition. Adorno's "On Popular Music" attempts to define pop music against what he calls "serious music,"[8] by which he means what we commonly think of as "classical" music today: the works of Beethoven, Mozart, and Brahms, for example. Notably, all of Adorno's examples of serious music are drawn from this European tradition of classical music, so one common (and accurate)

6. O'Riley, "OK O'Riley" (interview).
7. Yorke, "Fridge Buzz Now" (interview).
8. Adorno, "On Popular Music," 17.

criticism of Adorno's aesthetics of music is that he is deeply Eurocentric. My personal beef is not so much that Adorno fails to consider musical genres outside of the Western classical tradition, but that in judging pop and jazz against "serious music" he finds them fundamentally different and utterly lacking.

The most important aspect of this difference has to do with the relationship of individual parts of the music to the whole of a composition. In serious music, Adorno argues, "every detail derives its musical sense from the concrete totality of the piece which, in turn, consists of the life relationship of the details and never of a mere enforcement of a musical scheme."[9] Popular music, on the other hand, is characterized by "standardization," which Adorno calls its most fundamental characteristic.[10] In pop, unlike serious music, details of songs (e.g., choruses and verses) lack a significant relationship to the whole of the piece; there is no "concrete totality" to the song. In pop, "no stress is ever placed upon the whole as a musical event, nor does the structure of the whole ever depend upon the details," Adorno writes.[11] Although a pop song does possess some semblance of totality, in that its various elements fit together by virtue of melody, rhythm, and chord progression, each discrete element ultimately asserts itself irrespective of a total musical framework. This standardization of popular music extends from its "most general features to the most specific ones."[12]

The distinction between popular music and serious music has also been promoted historically by the "high/popular" culture divide, or a tendency to see certain forms of art and culture as inherently better than others. The notion of "high culture" has to do with the tastes of people who belong to richer or more powerful social classes. Popular culture, associated with middle or working classes, does not hold to the same values and standards, and is therefore often seen by conservative "high culture" critics as inferior in its artistic pursuits. Adorno, meanwhile, railed

9. Adorno, "On Popular Music," 19.
10. Adorno, "On Popular Music," 17.
11. Adorno, "On Popular Music," 19.
12. Adorno, "On Popular Music," 18.

against popular music because of its participation in the "culture industry," a form of aesthetic standardization due to capitalist appropriation.[13] The promotion of this high/popular disparity by cultural commentators went relatively unchallenged until the late twentieth century, when popular music began to be seen as a form worthy of study and scrutiny. And although pop music is taken more seriously by society than it used to be, the notion that it can be defined against classical music persists.

Whether or not we agree with Adorno that pop music should be considered separately from "serious music" due to standardization and repetition, most people can agree that there is something about pop music that does make it a category unto itself. Arthur Danto, in his influential article "The Artworld," writes about Andy Warhol's Brillo boxes: "What in the end makes the difference between a Brillo box and a work of art consisting of a Brillo box is a certain theory of art. It is the theory that takes it up into the world of art, and keeps it from collapsing into the real object which it is."[14] Warhol's Brillo boxes, Danto argues, are recognized as art even though they are in almost all ways identical to actual Brillo boxes one might have seen at the store in their heyday. What makes Warhol's boxes art is an understanding of art theory and history. A Brillo box is a Brillo box, but Warhol's Brillo box *is* a Brillo-box-as-art-object because the people who understand it as such hold to "a certain theory of art."

If an "artworld," with its concomitant history and theory, can be used to define art, it stands to reason that sub-worlds within art can be used to define subcategories of art. Perhaps, then, we can understand pop music in terms of a *popworld*. This possibility feels intuitively right to me as a fan, especially one who feels that critics like Adorno just don't "get it" when they claim that pop music is separate and inferior to classical music. After all, Adorno probably never went to a Beatles concert or had a friend lend him an Elvis record. The definition of pop music seems to be based on a kind of consensus, a shared belief in what historically constitutes pop.

13. Horkheimer and Adorno, *Dialectic of Enlightenment*, 120.
14. Danto, "Artworld," 581.

Those immersed in the popworld tend to agree that the act of Sting, Stewart Copeland, and Andy Summers playing their instruments together on a stage is a Police concert, no matter what style of music they are playing. Furthermore, we recognize as pop a number of artists who do not conform to some commonplace notions of popular music (repetitive, structured, short songs with prominent vocals): Joanna Newsom, a singer/songwriter who plays the harp and whose songs, influenced by medieval styles, stretch as long as twelve minutes, belongs to the pop world, and so does the Icelandic band Sigur Rós who play long, wordless, classically influenced pieces with electric guitars and drums, and so does the politically charged, electronic-beat driven music of British/Sri-Lankan rapper M.I.A. These artists have very little in common musically, but a music fan is likely to keep their albums next to each other in her collection.

The popworld is not wholly analogous to Danto's artworld, but the difference is illuminating. Danto writes, using an analogy from St. Augustine: "The artworld stands to the real world in something like the relationship in which the City of God stands to the Earthly City. Certain objects, like certain individuals, enjoy a double citizenship, but there remains . . . a fundamental contrast between artworks and real objects."[15] The difference between the artworld and the popworld, we might argue, is that *all* pop music enjoys double citizenship; pop-song "objects" simply *are* real-world objects, and pop music has a social function in peoples' real lives, not simply a rarified special realm of theory and history. Danto's theory of the artworld is associated with what he called, in an article and a book of the same name, the "transfiguration of the commonplace."[16] This is, I think, a great way to think about how music functions for most of us. To be a part of the pop music world is to participate socially, to integrate appreciation for pop music into one's daily life—the "real world." Take the Walkman and the iPod as examples—devices designed so as to make listening to music a seamless addition to day-to-day living.

15. Danto, "Artworld," 582.
16. Danto, "Transfiguration of the Commonplace," 148.

So, we might define pop music by what it is not (it is not "serious music"), and by its sociological functions (it is what people who "use" it say it is), but what about the way it sounds? Ladislav Račić correctly suggests that "the analysis of all the aspects of this musical genre should be performed on its own terms, and not by means of rules obtained by studying some other musical genres."[17] Therefore, he advocates defining pop music not by its form but by its style, or the "peculiar melodies, improvisations and the totality of the sound" it produces.[18] This totality differs from Adorno's notion of a formal totality in which all parts of a composition relate to a whole; Račić's totality is a stylistic one in which the parts of a composition cohere to create an overall sound or feeling without necessarily relating to each other in a formal sense.

But even style in pop is difficult to pin down. While a number of scholars of popular music have attempted to identify some characteristics of rock (in the sense of music in the tradition of the rock and roll genre), including noise, loudness, rhythm, and the importance of vocals, I hesitate to attempt a similar quest, for the simple reason that there seems to be too great a variety of musical expression permissible within what we recognize as pop music. If all pop music has to have a beat, what about Suzanne Vega's popular a capella single "Tom's Diner?" If it has to have lyrics, what about surf rock? Musical definitions are too easy to refute. The primacy of aurality may be one of pop's defining characteristics; Kofi Agawu, in his essay "The Challenge of Semiotics," writes that due to its nature as sound, "music exists only in performance."[19] Pop music, even when recorded, is rooted in the reality and immediacy of performance.

Ultimately, it seems we must look to extra-musical features of popular music in order to arrive at a definition. Račić writes that pop musicians are less concerned with particular musical elements than with creating songs which are "precious indicators of the

---

17. Račić, "Aesthetics of Rock Music," 201.
18. Račić, "Aesthetics of Rock Music," 202.
19. Agawu, "Challenge of Semiotics," 142.

intellectual preoccupations of rock lovers."[20] An investment in the pop world and a desire to create music in order to be interpreted by it—by these "rock lovers"—seem to be more apt criteria for a definition of pop music than any particular musical characteristics. We are always looking for songs that rule, and those who seek them tend to find them.

Once we have figured out what popular music is (and I'm not wholly certain we have), we can start thinking about how it is possible to evaluate or critique it, if such a thing is desirable. Certain realities are undeniable when it comes to the way pop critics, not to mention serious pop fans, evaluate music, even if most of us who are to some degree invested in the pop world might agree that the evaluation of pop is a fairly subjective enterprise. For example, an overwhelming majority of critics would agree that Nickelback are a bad band, whereas that same majority might agree that Slint are a good one. This resembles a critical consensus, but critics are not the only ones buying albums, because Nickelback is much more well-known and has sold many more thousands of albums than Slint. This ought to tell us something: in the pop music world, "critics" and "fans" probably disagree quite often, because if they did not, Slint would be more popular than Nickelback. (I am trying to imagine what a world in which this was true would look like.) Either the fans are wrong or the critics are—or the attempt to evaluate pop music is a doomed enterprise, ultimately a matter of personal taste which is utterly subjective.

This all does seem to make the evaluation of pop music a wholly subjective affair, which is unsatisfying both to critics who claim to know better and fans who fiercely love our favorite bands. There are other problems, too. If pop music is a performance-based genre, how can we evaluate what has come to be the basic unit of experiencing pop music, the recorded song? How does popular music criticism function? What, if anything, is the purpose of pop music criticism—not the kind found in academic journals, but the kind written for popular magazines, newspapers, and websites?

20. Račić, "Aesthetics of Rock Music," 202.

For years, music could only exist as an event, as a sound. It was something that could only be experienced "live" until the advent of sound recording in the early twentieth century. As such, the relationship of live music to recorded music parallels the relationship of spoken language to written language: once humans created a system of writing, our relationship to language altogether was significantly altered. But recorded music differs from written language because its modality does not change; whether one puts a Pearl Jam CD on the stereo or attends a Pearl Jam concert, one is listening. Recording is a kind of idealized performance by Agawu's accounting;[21] today, musicians can assemble for the sole purpose of making a recording rather than presenting a live performance for a live audience. In fact, rock bands can make whole albums without ever being in the same room. If one of pop's characteristics is the act of aural performance, how do we evaluate what has become the basic "unit" of pop music—the recorded song?

Agawu, writing about the performative nature of music, also mentions that its essence is play,[22] something that happens when people get together and explore making sounds together. What happens when the "language" of music—this living, changing, playing thing—is recorded, entombed on tape? Rhetorician Walter Ong calls written language "dead" oral language, arguing that "the paradox lies in the fact that the deadness of the text, its removal from the living human lifeworld, its rigid visual fixity, assures its endurance and its potential for being resurrected into limitless living contexts by a potentially infinite number of living readers."[23] The paradox of recorded *music* lies in the fact that the deadness of the *recording*, its removal from the living human lifeworld, its *recorded* fixity, assures its endurance and its potential for being resurrected into limitless living contexts by a potentially infinite number of living *listeners*. In essence, performance is recreated by pop recordings, and can be evaluated as such. Walter Benjamin, in "The Work of Art in the Age of Mechanical Reproduction" writes

21. Agawy, "Challenge of Semiotics," 142.
22. Agawu, "Challenge of Semiotics," 145.
23. Ong, *Orality and Literacy*, 80.

that "even the most perfect reproduction of a work of art is lacking in one element: its presence in time and space, its unique existence at the place where it happens to be."[24] Benjamin saw mechanical reproduction as the end of the "aura" of an original piece of art, but Andrew Goodwin argues that the "age of digital reproduction" actually allows everyone to own an "original" performance on record.[25]

As David E. W. Fenner writes, R. G. Collingwood saw "creativity" as the important feature of art: "The artist's expression, essentially the creative process itself, *is* the artwork. . . . The creative process and the art itself are most closely aligned."[26] In music, of course, the creative process of performance *is* the product. It will sometimes be vastly different, as in jazz or some "jam" bands, but even a rock band plays a slightly different show every night. The contemporary pop era is characterized by a desire to see a "behind-the-scenes" process *as* product, or process as central to the artistic experience: bands blogging or streaming live from the studio, the famous interview with Brian Wilson as he was working on *Smile,* filming the recording of an album (The Beatles in *Let It Be,* Wilco in *I Am Trying to Break Your Heart*), and so on. The pop world values the process of making pop music especially now that recordings are the basic unit of pop; in learning more about the process, we may be able to arrive at an evaluation of product. We like seeing inside that creative process because it is closer to what is still the vestigial basis of pop music: performance.

Just as Adorno separated "serious music" and popular music, Richard Meltzer separates serious music criticism (i.e., academic writing by scholars of aesthetics and philosophy) and popular music criticism (i.e., non-academic writing by non-scholars). Meltzer, who himself straddles those two traditions, sees the critical distance or disinterest of serious music criticism as its chief flaw. He writes (as you may recall from the very beginning of this book): "the art critic can never be epistemologically capable of describing

24. Benjamin, "Work of Art," 220.

25. Goodwin, "Sample and Hold," 35.

26. Fenner, *Introducing Aesthetics,* 76.

art by thinking *at* being, but must think *from* and *within* being. I have thus deemed it a necessity to describe rock 'n' roll by allowing my description to be itself a parallel artistic effort."[27] For Meltzer, rock and rock criticism are, if not inseparable, driven by common underlying properties. They are parallel artistic efforts, or even parts of the same artistic and social endeavor.

Meltzer argues that "rock is the only possible future for philosophy and art (and finally philosophy and art are historically interchangeable)."[28] The first part of this sentence is patently outrageous, but the second part goes remarkably far in articulating a theory of pop music criticism: "philosophy and art are historically interchangeable." This seems to be true, since the boundaries between professional critic, amateur appreciator, and pop artist, are not recognized, or least rendered unimportant, in pop music. As I said in my book *Sects, Love, and Rock & Roll:* "The very idea of a *fan* (short for *fanatic*) offers a clue about what drives any scene in the pop world: people's personal and social investment in it, or even, dare I say, their love."[29] As I said in the last chapter, the distinctions between roles in the pop world are blurry. Fans are self-styled critics, and identify so much with bands that they wish to be them, or pretend to be them, or become them by starting bands themselves. Critics are fans before anything else, and often (failed or amateur) musicians. Bands are fans of other bands and are amateur critics of themselves and of other bands. Roles overlap between the three groups, and each is equally capable of evaluating music.

If the fan/critic/artist divide is relatively unimportant in evaluating pop music—if it doesn't matter who is doing the evaluation—then what is the function of the rock critic? Benjamin writes that "the public must always be proved wrong, yet always feel represented by the critic."[30] And indeed pop fans often disagree with critics, but they need to believe the critic is simply attempting

27. Meltzer, *Aesthetics of Rock*, 7.

28. Meltzer, *Aesthetics of Rock*, 7.

29. Heng Hartse, *Sects, Love, and Rock & Roll*, 122.

30. Benjamin, "One-Way Street," 67.

an honest evaluation, the best anyone could do. Pop music does not recognize the same kind of critical separation—distance or disinterest—which art criticism does. Philosopher-critics tend to act with the assumption that they are, if not impartial, at least uniquely endowed judges of aesthetics, engaged in what Benjamin called the "literary battle"[31] in a way that ordinary people are not. Aesthetic evaluation of pop, perhaps because of its social basis, does *not* recognize this critic/"regular person" division when it comes to imbuing the music with meaning. In a sense, pop cannot be evaluated in the elitist way that other types of music can be and have been, because the pop world is not amenable to such a division. John Dewey emphasized the interaction between the perceiver of art and the art object, talked about art as a unified and complete experience, and believed in the importance of the experience of the common person,[32] and indeed, in pop, the common person—the fan—is no less important than the critic in determining music's worth.

If pop evaluation is not elitist—if pop music is best evaluated by people who are invested in it and not by those who maintain some critical distance—what is the function of *professional* pop criticism? Surely the kind of highbrow, academic criticism Meltzer rejects is just as socially mediated. Why do people like me sometimes get paid (not very much, I should stress) to evaluate popular music, and why does anyone bother to read album reviews? There seem to be more questions than answers. Traditional models of evaluating the aesthetic good because something moral is at stake seem to break down. Is it my moral duty to explain why NoMeans-No is a brilliant punk band and why they are better than, say, Sum 41? Even if we want to believe that evaluation of pop should not be completely subjective, within the pop world, it is difficult to imagine that there is something morally superior that one artist holds above another.

Veteran pop critic Robert Christgau offers one implicit answer to the question of rock criticism's purpose in the name of his

31. Benjamin, "One-Way Street," 66.
32. See Sawyer, *Group Creativity*, ch. 4.

long-running album-review column, "Consumer Guide," which was published by the *Village Voice* for many years. Christgau's title implies that he offers advice on whether music fan/consumers ought to spend their money on certain albums the way *Consumer Reports* offers advice about buying blenders or minivans. Common sense tells us that album reviews are, in part, advice about how to spend our money—or nowadays, at least which songs to stream, which will in theory generate a few cents for the artist.

In the end, the purpose of pop criticism may not be so much consumer guide or detached critical analysis; Simon Frith argues that the purpose of pop music reviews "isn't so much representing music to the public (the public to the musician) as creating a knowing community."[33] Pop critics, then, represent one part of constituting what literary scholar Stanley Fish calls "the interpretive community," without which no meaning or value can be determined.[34] The most famous quote about pop criticism, which we have discussed already, is that "writing about music is like dancing about architecture." The implication, of course, is that rock criticism is pointless, a waste of time. This is not only uncharitable toward critics, but untrue from a pop world-perspective. Critics may not be the ultimate arbiters of meaning or value for pop music, but they are one important source of determining whether and how pop music matters in the everyday lives of the people who care about it.

As I write this, I am listening to *Volta*, an album by the Icelandic artist Björk, long considered an artist who pushes the boundaries of popular music. But to distinguish Björk as somehow being almost non-pop seems a misunderstanding of the aesthetics of pop, a music whose "aesthetic value," Theodore Gracyk writes, "is a function of its use by appropriately knowledgeable listeners."[35] *Volta* features guest appearances by artists who are not considered pop musicians: free jazz drummer Chris Corsano, Congolese folk group Konono No. 1, Malian kora player Toumani Diabaté,

33. Frith, *Performing Rites*, 67.
34. Fish, *Is There a Text?*
35. Gracyk, "Valuing and Evaluating," 215.

Chinese pipa player Min Xiao-Fen. The BBC's Louis Pattison calls the album "outsider sounds carried into the mainstream through Björk's sheer sense of vision."[36] But adding non-traditional instruments to popular music, or employing people not traditionally considered pop musicians, does not fundamentally change what pop music is or whether anyone likes it. Neither people nor sounds can determine the way the music is defined or evaluated. In the end, it is only the listeners, the lovers, of music who can do so. Good music? We know it when we see it. And in the case of this album, anyway, I am happy to report that it does, indeed, rule.

36. Pattison, review of *Volta*.

(Confession of Faith)

I believe in rock songs more than church songs.
I believe in rock shows more than sermons.

I believe in three chords and the truth,
And also many more chords and many more truths.

I believe in God more than I believe in rock and roll,
But I believe in God because of rock and roll.

Attempts at Dancing about Architecture

The word "essay" comes from the French verb *essayer*, which means "to try" or "to attempt." I don't know if what I write about music truly counts as essays, because that word is so overused in my line of work (teaching writing to university students) that its meaning has become occluded, but I do regard the writing I've done about it over the last twenty years as attempts to pin down something elusive and ineffable. What follows here, then, are various essays—*attempts*—at dancing about architecture—on a variety of themes that are almost impossible to capture. I used to think language was the most important and valuable tool we had for making meaning, but after twenty years of writing about things that matter very much to me, I am no longer certain of this. When I look at these pieces, I am not always sure if what I meant to mean has been meant, as it were. But I have tried to write about some ineffable things here: hope, faith, loss, transcendence, and the self. These are things that feel very difficult to explain, but the best we can do is to try, and there can be an awful lot of joy in the trying. Like most of what I write, many of these pieces are concerned with the twin ineffables of music and religious faith, or even music and God: two things that seem very difficult to put words to, but that have always seemed, to me, worth trying to talk about as much as possible.

FAITH

One of my preoccupations as a writer-about-music has been what is called "Christian music." (In fact, I wrote an entire book about it about ten years ago.) This is a genre, if it can be called one, that is produced by and for evangelical Christians, mainly, and it is a genre that a lot of people feel (even those who make it and listen to it) uncomfortable with for that very reason. In this section are three (or four-ish) pieces. The first is a two-part piece about Sufjan Stevens, with each part written ten years apart. Stevens has been an important figure in the "Christian music" world despite clearly never intending to be a part of it, and is the only musician featured in this section who is not also an ordained clergyperson of some stripe. The next is about the band Luxury, who may have inadvertently stumbled into Christian rock in the 1990s but took a sharp turn away from it soon thereafter, even though they continue making deeply spiritual rock and roll. (I once tried to write an article about them called "Luxury: The Only Christian Band," which I could not finish, but which, I think you'll agree, is apt, given how many members of the band are ordained priests.) This section ends with an interview I did with a man improbably named Slim Moon, who runs one of the most respected independent record labels of all time, Kill Rock Stars, and who, also improbably, is also an ordained Unitarian minister.

All Things Go: How Sufjan Stevens Changed What It Means to Make Christian Music

If someone asked, I would say that I was born again. I would look you right in the eye and say it.

—SUFJAN STEVENS, IN A 2005 INTERVIEW
WITH *PLAN B* MAGAZINE

2005 was very much the year of Sufjan Stevens in the world of American popular music. His fifth album, *Illinois* (or *Sufjan Stevens Invites You To: Come On Feel the ILLINOISE*) was, according to the website Metacritic, the most favorably reviewed album released all year.[1] He sold out five consecutive nights at the Bowery Ballroom in New York City, and played Carnegie Hall. Stevens's music could be read about in all the major music magazines, was hard for independent record stores to keep in stock, and could always be found on evangelical pastors' iPods. Yes: Sufjan Stevens is not just the most lauded musician of 2005, but also a real life Christian, and a high-church one at that (in an interview, he described his Episcopal congregation as "Anglo-Catholic"[2]). And it is his music, in part, that perhaps permanently changed the idea of what "Christian music" can be. (Pop culture critic Jeffrey Overstreet declared, of Stevens's music: "The wall is down. There is no

1. Metacritic, "Illinois."
2. Stevens, interview by Noel Murray.

more reason for the Christian music industry to exist."[3]) How could this thirty-year-old short story writer from Michigan, with a slight lisp and a Muslim name (which his parents chose after a brief association with the new religious movement Subud), who plucks a banjo plaintively and whose voice is rarely raised above the volume that might be reserved for a serious discussion about anthropology, become the savior of "Christian music"?

There are reasons for Stevens's (deserved) mantle of leadership in this new Christian music movement, perhaps the most important being that this is not a movement, nor is it, strictly speaking, Christian music. You see, for about thirty-five years, something has existed called Contemporary Christian Music (CCM), something initially conceived by hippie rockers who wanted to sing about Jesus that eventually became a multimillion-dollar industry based on record companies and marketing firms who were experts at selling a particular idea about music to evangelical Christians. That idea was: *here is some pop music that sounds a lot like what you might hear on any radio station, or on MTV, or your friends' record collections, but instead of being about romantic love or having a good time, is about God, and is devoid of swear words, drug references, and sex.*

CCM was and is many things—a "safe" alternative to morally debauched rock or rap, a way to praise the Lord to a funky beat, well-crafted songs about love and spiritual longing made by evangelicals who want to make songs for Christians—but it has almost always, since its inception, existed in a cultural silo. CCM, though it has no flagship style, is considered a genre from a marketing perspective, complete with a readymade target market—"people of faith." From time to time, CCM has produced "crossover" artists who eventually sign with major labels who market their music in places other than Christian bookstores to varying degrees of success, including Amy Grant and Michael W. Smith in the late 1980s, Jars of Clay and Sixpence None the Richer in the mid-1990s, and Switchfoot and Underoath in the early 2000s. Most "crossover" artists attained a significant degree of success in the Christian market

3. Overstreet, reply to "Sufjan Stevens?!?" (forum post).

before making the leap, and each has faced unique challenges from their evangelical fan base ("they've abandoned their faith!") and "secular" pop fans and critics ("Christians playing rock music? *Please!*"). Significantly, almost all of these crossover artists are affiliated with what are called "major labels," large corporations that are more in the business of shifting units and pleasing shareholders than delivering artistically relevant music.

But Sufjan Stevens did not cross over; he didn't have to. From his 2003 album *Michigan*, Stevens captured the ears of serious music listeners, Christian or not, and did so without participating in any of the practices that create the possibility of crossover. Stevens has never been signed to a Christian record label; his records are all released on an independent label, Asthmatic Kitty Records, which he co-founded. His music has not been sold in Christian bookstores, advertised in Christian publications, or played at Christian festivals. Stevens's lyrics are not Jesus smackdowns, they're beautiful portraits of humanity: hope, love, joy, peace, pain, murder, sickness, alien invasions, unemployment, history, road trips, faith. "Casimir Pulaski Day" from *Illinois* is a tender story of young lovers whose relationship is cut short by parental disapproval and cancer. The song is bathed in prayer and hope, but ends with death and resigned thankfulness, as Stevens praises God even though "He takes / and He takes / and He takes." The chilling and ethereal "John Wayne Gacy, Jr." is a heartbreaking ballad about the sadistic serial killer that ends with Stevens alone, in a wavering tenor, claiming "in my best behavior / I am really just like him." The song is terrifying in its depravity and beauty, and nakedly blunt and personal in its assertion of the doctrine of original sin.

It's not just that Stevens is a critical success, as if that somehow proves that "the world" can learn to respect music about God as long as it's as cool as "secular" music; it's that he has made music with integrity from the beginning, never adding or subtracting the word "Jesus" from a song to appease someone, never hawking minivans or snowboards with his music, never bending a vision of God-glorifying art to be less "worldly" for the Christian market or less Jesusy for the secular rock market. Sufjan Stevens has proven that CCM is over (if we want it); as he and his chorus sing on "Chi-cago": "All things go." Stevens's artistic success is proof that people who seek God don't have to settle for ghettoized, bowdlerized pop music. This non-movement is ever on the move, and people who care about both God and music don't have to be left behind.

How Not to Listen to Sufjan Stevens

Sufjan Stevens released his most lauded studio album, *Carrie & Lowell*, in 2015. It's a record inspired primarily by the death of his estranged mother, and as such, it's raw, beautiful, and delicate. *Carrie & Lowell* is only Stevens's fifth proper album, but the prolific Brooklyn-based artist has been making folk, rock, electronic, and neoclassical music for many years, music that's always informed by his Christian faith, even if not always explicitly so.

Carrie & Lowell is Stevens's most personal and intimate album, providing a window into his grief; into his love for and abandonment by his mother; and into his journey through all kinds of unhealthy coping mechanisms in the wake of loss. There are hints at substances, sex, and suicidal thoughts throughout the album, but they are treated with a light melancholy, evoking the early records of Elliott Smith and the more tender ballads of Simon and Garfunkel.

Carrie & Lowell marks two new directions for Stevens. First, every song is an exercise in restraint and economy—the exceptions are the ambient instrumental outros on a handful of tracks, but even these feel necessary given the ethereal, somber mood of the record. Second, Stevens has abandoned the high-concept artifice of his other work and its epic themes: American history, the Chinese zodiac, the outsider artist and self-proclaimed prophet Royal Robertson, and the Brooklyn–Queens Expressway, to name a few. *Carrie & Lowell* does have a concept, but it is one taken directly from the singer's experience. As Stevens told *Pitchfork*: "This is not my art project; this is my life."[1]

It is difficult to identify a "standout" track on this album. All are short, gentle, and sparse. The first, "Death with Dignity," and the last, "Blue Bucket of Gold," are among the most melodically arresting, but most of the songs paint similar landscapes: memories of Carrie mix with feelings of regret and confusion ("I should've wrote a letter / explaining what I feel," from "Should Have Known Better") and questions about the meaning of suffering ("My prayer has always been love / what did I do to deserve this?" Stevens pleads on "Drawn to the Blood"). There aren't "answers" to grief and loss provided here, though at times the lyrics make clear the source of Stevens's will to carry on: the hope in the next generation, represented by his niece; friendship and romantic love; and his faith in Christ.

Aside from *Carrie & Lowell*'s artistic merits, its uncomfortably naked premise offers a chance to reflect on evangelicals' embrace of Stevens and his music. If it is increasingly clear that Stevens is not, in fact, the poster boy for hipster Christianity we might have once taken him for, can Christians continue to receive his music as a gift instead of as a "statement" about the integration of art and faith?

Evangelicals first began paying attention to Stevens after the release of his 2004 album, *Seven Swans*. While many were aware that his previous album, *Michigan*, touched on spiritual themes (for example, "Vito's Ordination Song," written for his Presbyterian pastor friend Vito Aiuto, also of the band The Welcome Wagon), *Seven Swans* was both biblical and devotional, with songs about Abraham and Isaac and the Transfiguration as well as more worshipful tracks such as "To Be Alone with You." The album cemented Stevens's place as a respected indie-folk singer-songwriter and a serious Christian voice within mainstream music. Indie-rock tastemakers loved *Seven Swans*, and Christian music fans had a guy on the inside, it seemed.

---

1. Stevens, "True Myth" (interview).

But it doesn't quite honor Stevens's own story for evangelical Christians to label him as "one of us." He did, for a time, attend Hope College, a Michigan school affiliated with the Reformed Church in America denomination, but I'm hard-pressed to think of other formal involvement he's had with evangelical institutions. To be sure, his sense of art-making and creativity are inextricably bound up with his faith, but not in the way that many evangelicals have done so.

In a blog post presumably written while recording *Carrie & Lowell*, Stevens heartily recommends the 1983 book *The Gift: Imagination and the Erotic Life of Property*. In it, essayist and cultural critic Lewis Hyde defends the value of making art simply as a gift to the public, an act that's increasingly radical in a culture governed by money and trade. In his post, Stevens likens art-making to the act of Communion, wherein we receive the body of Christ as absolute gift. Stevens writes:

> To objectify art is to measure its commercial value and squander its transcendental powers of benevolence. Reciprocity demeans art; or, rather, it functions to incarcerate its powers, to judge it for its charity. Like putting Mother Teresa on trial, or in prison, for the crime of compassion. On the contrary, perfect art, as a perfect gift (without ulterior motive, without gain, without compensation) courageously gives itself over to the world asking nothing in return. Do I engage with my work as a father cultivates his child, with loving-kindness, with fierce enrichment, with awe and wonder, with unconditional love, with absolute sacrifice? I make this my impossible objective.[2]

Stevens's vision of music-making here may illustrate why he's sidestepped the world of Christian music altogether. Though it has changed over the years, Christian pop music has usually had a goal: to evangelize or to aid worship or to otherwise edify believers. There is usually a statement to be made, a position to be taken. Stevens, on the other hand, seems to have no interest in doing

2. Stevens, "The Gift" (blog post).

anything but following his artistic whims, creating beauty for its own sake. These whims sometimes lead to uncomfortable places— places that listeners, Christian and otherwise, are not always comfortable going: avant-garde symphonic pieces, twenty-five-minute hip-hop dance songs, lyrics that depict sexually ambiguous desire, and, now, deeply personal grief.

Carrie & Lowell is an achievement—many reviews have called it Stevens's best album—in part because it doesn't feel like a statement of anything other than life experience, artfully rendered. And here is where Stevens's longtime Christian fans are most challenged, in the best way: Will we objectify Stevens and his music by demanding that he stand in for a Christian aesthetic? Will we continue to use him as proof that Christians can crack the code of culture and use its tools? Or will we simply receive Stevens's vulnerable songwriting for the gift that it is?

In another blog post from the same period as the one quoted above, Stevens wrote a short, impassioned paragraph advocating "all manners of love at any cost. Any other option defiles the insurmountable reverence due all creation, immeasurable in bounty and beauty, incomparable in awe. The world is abundant, against all odds. My prayer has always been love."[3] *Carrie & Lowell* is acknowledged as an album made in response to tragedy and grief. But it is one that responds to this bounty, beauty, and awe of creation, the extravagant gift of all that is. And it responds not with platitudes or arguments or artifice, but with the shimmering, honest offering of itself.

3. Stevens, "All Come from Somewhere" (blog post).

Luxury: Transcendence and Transgression

I am so interested in religion and in music and in art. Why
do people feel the need to restrict themselves, to be one-
dimensional? Perhaps it is easier. Always a priest or always a
nurse or always a mother. But who is always anything? Always a
Christian is the only always worth being.

—LEE BOZEMAN, IN A 2013 POST ON HIS BLOG

1.

In 2014, the philosopher Stephen H. Webb wrote a review of Christopher Partridge's book *The Lyre of Orpheus: Popular Music, the
Sacred, and the Profane* for the religious magazine *First Things*. The
review was titled "Can Christian Music Be Real Rock and Roll?" I
was interested. Unfortunately, I can't muster the time or attention
such a book probably deserves. Popular music and the sacred (and
indeed the profane, to be honest) are pretty interesting to me, but
I have trouble getting at these things in an academic way, since I
already have an academic job in another field. I'd rather dig into
popular music itself and see what the sacred and the profane are
doing there. One of the notions Webb touches on in his review,
which I assume he is faithfully interpreting from Partridge's book,
is this: "Rock is essentially transgressive. Christianity upholds a
sacred order that excludes the profane. Therefore, contemporary

Christian music cannot be true rock and roll, because it is 'unable to establish a credible presence in [rock's] profane affective space.'"[1]

This seems untrue in my experience, and not only because it is impossible for me to disentangle my experience of Christianity from my experience of rock music. (You can blame dc Talk's "Jesus Freak," among many other songs, for this.) It also seems untrue because one of the most badass rock and roll bands I've ever heard comprises 60 percent clergy.

2.

I once sent a postcard to an Orthodox priest who ministers at a small mission in suburban Texas. I'd bought it at a used bookshop in Bellingham, Washington; the image was a photograph of the stained-glass art on an old Scandinavian church. This seemed a much better way to contact the priest, known to his parishioners as Fr. David Bozeman, and to me as Lee Bozeman, than by email or phone or any other method.

3.

The most obvious touchstone or comparison for Lee Bozeman's music is Morrissey; the band Bozeman has led, off and on again for twenty-five years, sounds a lot like the Smiths would have, if they had been contemporaneous with Radiohead and had embraced punk rock. Bozeman's aesthetic is unashamedly Morrisseyan, from lyrics to melodies to album artwork (for example, most of his projects feature album art of faded glamor photos from bygone eras). Bozeman's lyrics and melodies are as dramatic as Morrissey's, though his voice is higher and he does not sing off key.

1. Webb, "Real Rock and Roll?"

4.

One gets the sense that Morrissey, for all the earnest poses he strikes in concert, is perhaps not entirely serious when he sings melodramatic religious songs like "I Have Forgiven Jesus" and "Satan Rejected My Soul." One does not feel the same flippancy in Bozeman's work; there is more at stake. Where the Smiths' "Please, Please, Please, Let Me Get What I Want" is followed by a sprightly guitar solo, Bozeman's "Jardim Gramacho," which expresses the same sentiment, ends in ominous, echoing piano chords. Both are pleas for desires to be granted: the former is a tossed-off wish to the ether, the other a prayer to Jesus Christ.

Like I said: more at stake.

5.

The centerpiece of Bozeman's *oeuvre* is probably "The Wedding Feast of the Lamb" from the album *Love & Affection*, which he released under the name All Things Bright and Beautiful. It brings together most of the preoccupations of his songwriting: sex, family, the social obligations people have to each other, liturgy, the apocalypse, and the afterlife. The lyrics are beautiful and unsettling, and worth quoting at length: after waking from his marital bed and walking to work, the speaker gets lost in an internal reverie, ruminating on his own character, until the final astonishing verse.

> I'll die smiling, turn toward heaven
> Sing some old songs and claim my crown
> Then I'll go to find someone I've been waiting
> To talk with since I read *The Habit of Being*
> She'll tell me her story of sorrow and suffering
> She'll tell me it's so sad the way we've been acting
> For we are surrounded by thousands of liars
> That sing lovely songs in a river of fire
> That flows from the hand of the Father

The verse is about meeting Flannery O'Connor in the world to come, but the song is about a lot more than that; it's about living on earth as it is in heaven, to put it in simpler terms than I should. To hear a man sing so matter-of-factly about the end of the world is all the more affecting when you consider that he might actually believe it.

6.

I have tried multiple times to pitch stories about Bozeman and Luxury to some magazines, but neither I nor editors ever seem to be able to make them work. For my part, I find it difficult to explain to non-believers why this band is so earth-shakingly good; for editors, I suspect the premise is too much of a novelty: Lee Bozeman, and his guitarist and brother Jamey Bozeman, and the band's bassist, Chris Foley, are all Orthodox priests. Priests! In a rock band! WTF, LOL, right? What I could not explain in my pitches and can barely articulate now is how right and natural it feels for Luxury to be (a) a sincere, wounded rock band who sing mostly about sex, death, and decadence, and also (b) a group of non-ironically bearded men who spend their non-rock-and-roll time performing liturgies, administering sacraments, and providing pastoral care.

7.

I believe, for some reason, that beautiful rock music, played sincerely and well, is itself a form of love, a kenosis, a self-giving. Perhaps this is because I am an evangelical who went to Jars of Clay concerts for years before I ever went to so much as an Ash Wednesday Mass. Rock bands, not prayer books or liturgies, were the ticket to God for me and my generation. So it has taken me a lot longer to understand traditional Christian practices—like religious vocations and sacraments and rote prayers—and to accept that there is also love in these things, which once felt cold and empty to me.

8.

I think about this claim that rock music is somehow inherently transgressive, that it cannot succeed if it does not in some way kick against the pricks of authority, and especially that stand-in for inflexible authoritarianism, "religion," and I find myself agreeing with Webb, who at the end of his piece writes: "The alternative to transgression is transcendence, not docile submission to social order."[2] You can rage against the machine all you want, or you can look for a way to rise above both the rage and the machine, without denying either.

Because in a secular age, transcendence *is* transgression. To write songs that yearn for "something more"—not in a vague, pie-in-the-sky way, but in a sacramental, earthy, no-ideas-but-in-things way, a way that demands access to Paul Éluard's "other world" that is "in this one"[3]—is to violate the spirit of the times which demands there is no such thing as spirit.

9.

Exhibit A of the above: Luxury's 2004 song "I Have Been Everywhere the Grass is Green, I Have Seen All There is to See" from their fourth album, *Health and Sport*. It's a soaring, pounding, relentless song, driven by two chords and frenetic drum fills, sung—again, I am sorry I am emphasizing this punchline so much but I just want you to remember—by guys who dress like fourth-century monks. Its few brief verses seem to depict a world-weary dissatisfaction: "though they tried to give me sight / all I have seen is artificial light," one line goes. By the end, there's some sense of peace in grasping at things like family and kindness, but its chorus,

2. Webb, "Real Rock and Roll?"
3. Llewelyn, *Margins of Religion*, 307–8.

sung in a resigned croon by Lee Bozeman with desperate, straining backing vocals by his brother, underscores a desperation and
yearning that is missing from most allegedly "transgressive" rock
and roll:

> I'd love to believe
> There was something for me
> Where we could just live
> Like living should be
> I'd love to believe!

This straining toward a so-far unachievable paradise is as musical as it is lyrical. The song threatens to break under its own
weight, and doesn't feel fully resolved (really, it doesn't ever feel
fully resolved) until Jamey Bozeman's final vocal slide on that last
"be-leeeeeaaave!"

10.

I have the feeling that the wrongest thing you can say about popular
music—apart from the canard that writing about it is like "dancing
about architecture"—is that it has to in some sense be "bad." My
response to the question "why should the Devil have all the good
music?" has always been: does *he though*? Sure, a lot of the best
rock music in history has been shocking, or profane, or angry, or
sensual, but above all, so much of it has been so *beautiful*. There is
no need to restrict rock and roll to a one-dimensional caricature
of 1980s sex-drugs-and-misogyny hair metal. The alleged badas-
sery of much popular music strikes me as an utterly boring and
conventional rehashing of tired tropes about rebellion, excess, and
social deviance.

Maybe this is just me, but I'd rather listen to a band that makes
me flirt with the idea that everything in my life is meaningless, a
chasing after the wind, and that I should sell everything I own and
give it to the poor, and that proclaims the most transgressive thing
is to receive, remake, and offer up what is given—whether as rock
and roll, or as the Eucharist itself.

Superfluous Beauty: An Interview with Slim Moon

In the summer of 2004, I got an incredibly intimidating email that was only eight words long, in all lowercase letters:

"can you come to oly for an interview?"

This doesn't sound like a big deal, maybe, but the email was from Slim Moon, founder and president of what is probably the hippest, indiest indie record label in the world, Kill Rock Stars. They were looking for a new promo person, and I thought I might fit the bill, coming as I was off a couple of years of working for my college radio station. But when the email came, I chickened out, scared that I wasn't cool enough for the label that launched the careers of Elliott Smith, Sleater-Kinney, Gossip, and the Decemberists. One of the things that scared me was I was worried they would find out I went to a Christian college and think I was too square or conservative to work there. I decided I wouldn't even go to the interview, sent a half-hearted excuse about not wanting to move to Olympia, and enrolled in grad school in California instead.

I'll never know if the KRS job would have been good for me, but I was surprised and intrigued when I found out that Slim Moon had quit the indie rock world to go to (Unitarian) seminary. I was even more surprised and intrigued when I interviewed him in 2015 about it and he told me he goes to Christian worship concerts for fun. Some time after this interview, Moon returned to helming KRS, but delving into his history with rock, religion, sobriety, and the mysteries of God was rewarding, and now I feel like I probably could have gotten that job after all.

Joel: Could you talk a little bit about maybe just a
         short version of what you were doing with Kill
         Rock Stars and how your trajectory led you from
         there to where you are now?

Slim: I guess you could say I was one of those kids who
         always felt like I didn't belong when I was a kid
         and then, in high school . . . I found my first sort
         of belonging actually in gaming, like role-playing
         games. When I was sixteen, I discovered under-
         ground music through college radio and then
         I started going to see shows. People who don't
         know about underground music probably don't
         know that we don't call them concerts, we call
         them shows.

         I started going to see shows and then I started
         drinking and I started drinking really heavily.
         And then I dropped out of high school. I ran
         away from home and I lived on the street, but
         I got really, really involved in the local music
         scene. When I got my life somewhat back to-
         gether, I reconnected with my family and went to
         college . . . I got a GED and went to college.

         I moved to Olympia, Washington, to go to col-
         lege, but the real reason I moved there was not
         because of the college. The college was cool, but
         I'd barely even researched the college. I just went
         there because they accepted my application and
         all my favorite bands in the Pacific Northwest
         were from Olympia. It seems as if the music
         scene there had something special going on and
         I really moved there to be a part of it. The Seattle
         scene was OK, but the Olympia scene seemed
         even cooler, and it was.

I was in several bands over the next few years. I got kicked out of college and I also quit drinking. I was in a bunch of bands and I made a lot of friends who lived there who had cool bands and a lot of friends whose bands came through town and played there.

I got a job through a low-income, at-risk teens program. I got a temporary training job at a state agency. I was supposed to only be there for a month, but they ended up keeping me for six years. I got several promotions, then I saw I had extra money. I grew up pretty—not that well-off, especially in our early years. I had never expected to have, like, a middle-class income, and then I had a middle-class income at twenty-three and so I decided, instead of moving somewhere nice or buying a car, I just decided to start putting out records.

My intention was to just put out spoken word records. Although I've been in some bands, the thing I was most connected to then was doing spoken word as a performance art, which is somewhat like poetry. I was just going to do spoken word records and I did a couple of seven-inches, but then I got talked into doing a compilation. The compilation had a bunch of my friends' bands from Olympia and some friends' bands from elsewhere around the country.

One of the tracks on that album was with my friends in Nirvana, and essentially they gave me the song just before they turned famous. Our compilation came out and then their album came out a week or two after the compilation and immediately did really well. They sold ten million albums, but 25,000 people bought my compilation, which was enough to give me the seed money to put out more records and then from there, I just did that for fifteen years.

That's how we got started. There's more to the story—we then put out some records associated with the Riot Grrrl movement like Bikini Kill and Sleater-Kinney and Huggy Bear. The highlights that people usually hit are the Riot Grrrl bands and then later the Elliot Smith . . .

Joel: and the Decemberists.

Slim: . . . and then later the Decemberists. Oh, and Gossip, yeah. Those are the ones that at least nipped at the mainstream consciousness.

Joel: Does it bother you that that's what people always bring up? Because you did a lot more than that, right?

Slim: No, it doesn't bother me. One of the things that bothers me is that . . . I think there's some really terrific records that we put out, bands that we worked with who, I think, deserved more attention and so, I'm frustrated that some bands are sort of forgotten to history or that a lot of young people who probably would really like their music just never even get a chance to hear it.

Joel: I know from some radio interviews you did that you started exploring spirituality somewhere in there while you were still doing the label. Eventually you felt this need or this calling toward the ministry. Was that something that you felt a conflict about in some way? Did you feel you needed to quit what you were doing? How did that transition come about?

Slim:	When I was ten, my parents got divorced and my dad got sober. He was in Alcoholics Anonymous and over the next few years, he was really engaged not only with the meetings and the fellowship, but he engaged with it really intellectually so he found some of the books that were credited as having influenced the writers of the Alcoholics Anonymous basic text, the *Big Book*. He read William James and he read a bunch of things, but I ended up reading his books.
	The Varieties of Religious Experience was the first religious book I ever read and I was about twelve at that point. I read *Surprised by Joy* and *Mere Christianity* by C. S. Lewis before I read the Narnia books and then I read the Narnia books and the Space Trilogy.
Joel:	So you weren't one of those kids who was, like, you get to the end, and you're like, "wait a minute, this was Christian all along!" You actually knew.
Slim:	Yeah. From that point on, I had an interest, but I guess the other thing I should say is I was raised completely unchurched. My parents didn't go to church and only one my four grandparents went to church.
Joel:	Wow.
Slim:	I know. I grew up thinking that that was normal and the church people were weird and that was in Montana. Now I know that in a place like Montana, I realize that was actually unusual.
Joel:	So you had this experience of reading these books, but not really being a part of that kind of a culture.

Slim: It was completely intellectual. It was not any culture at all. When I was in my punk rock days and when I was in my drinking days, I had no religious practice and no spiritual practice whatsoever, but me and my best friend would argue with people all the time about anything. We didn't toe the line of what it's supposed to mean to be in a punk rock community.

Any time anybody would say that religion is dumb or that atheism is the only rational standpoint or viewpoint, I would always argue in favor of religion or in favor of the existence of God, but it was just completely intellectual. It wasn't in my heart, there wasn't any practice.

But then I followed in my father's footsteps when I was thirty. He got sober when he was thirty. When I was thirty, I went to rehab and got clean. I think that's when a life of addiction or life of alcoholism is really starting to wear you out or cause a lot of problems in your life. Then, the 12 Steps, I did the 12 Steps and I guess . . . because of tradition, I'm not supposed to say what fellowship I'm a part of, but my interpretation is I feel like it's OK for me to say that I did work the 12 Steps.

In the 12 Steps, for example, the third step is you make a decision that you're turning your life over to God and then say in the tenth step, you have a regular practice of prayer and meditation. From then on, I leaned in and finally tried to figure out, well, what does God mean in my life? What is God doing in my life and in the world?

Also, the 12 Steps, they lay out a way of processing things in a way of attempting to grow that has been a really good spiritual practice for me in terms of doing a regular inventory, doing a big inventory, and sharing that inventory, looking at my character assets and defects, sharing that with other people, and then asking, trying to become entirely ready and asking God from a very humble position to help me with those character defects.

The last bit I'll say about the 12 Steps is the reason, the impetus that moved me from just the 12 Steps over to church was that when I got to the twelfth step which says, having had a spiritual awakening, we try to carry this, the message, to others, and I couldn't . . . for me, when I worked that step a second time, I realized that, having had a spiritual awakening it was authentic. I had had a spiritual awakening and that having had a spiritual awakening, I couldn't only carry the message just to people who have the same problem as me.

The only thing I could do in good conscience is carry the message to the world to whatever my limited capacity. It just didn't seem right to me to just keep it to one population because I feel like I learned the message of transformation and grace that isn't just applicable to people with compulsive chemical addictions.

Joel: Did you feel like the 12 Steps led pretty naturally to UU? I personally don't have a lot of experience with Unitarianism, but you know the stereotypes, like, well, it's just for people who like the idea of going to church, which is probably an unfair characterization.

Slim:
I think that might be fair in some of our churches. Here's the thing. The thing I love about Unitarian Universalism is that we can have theological diversity and that's something I love about the 12 Steps, is that as its practice, you can have Buddhists and Christians and Muslims and atheists and pagans still agree on the language where we say higher power as we understand it and really, really help each with real significant, meaningful spiritual concepts. Not just the generic support that you might give to a friend, but real spiritual support, and at its best, Unitarian Universalism can do that and that does happen in all of our churches, but it varies depending on the leadership whether it's done well or not. I am attracted to that, to the theological diversity.

The other thing is, even though I said I have no church background, I have this tiny, tiny bit of church background. My grandmother had been a Methodist, but when her youngest child went to college, he got involved with a Unitarian campus ministry and so she went to the Unitarian church with him. At the Methodist church, the women had to wash the dishes. She went to his Unitarian church and they used paper plates and they threw out the dishes and she said, "OK, I'm becoming a Unitarian." She switched to Unitarian in the seventies and has been Unitarian ever since.

That was the closest thing I had to a tradition. When I decided to start going to church in my forties that seemed like a logical place because I had good memories of it from when I was eleven.

Joel:
I've heard you describe a couple of times the idea of like a call or a calling and maybe you already

described that, but was it as simple as just saying, *hey, I've found this, the thing that really worked for me. I want to tell people about it?* Was there any kind of mystical side to it?

Slim: Yeah. For me, I think it's important to be able to not get caught up in language that divides us, so a lot of times, when I preach, I won't necessarily talk about God or whatever. Because there are lots of Unitarians who have really bad experience from their childhood and they'd rather think of something like spirit of light than think of the word God because the word God has been so sort of toxified from the theology that they were exposed to as a kid.

Just to put it in my own language, in the language I think of it as in my head, is that by doing that third step, turning my will and my life over to the care of God, the proof for me—I guess this is mystical, but the proof to me of God working in my life—is just how everything changed after that and that I had tried every single thing I could think of to change my habits and my mental afflictions and my sticking points and nothing I thought of worked, but when I said yes to that step and I decided to do it to the best of my ability as honestly as I could, it really did change my life, and I've seen that happen over and over and over for people.

I have the highest respect for my atheist friends who say that they just can't do that because they can't see any proof, but I have also seen atheist friends of mine get talked into, "Why don't you just act as if you believe in God and why don't you just pray for a while just to see what happens?" and watch them experience changes in their life and in their perception that have caused them to go, "wow, this thing I didn't believe in, the proof is actually just inside me, and how it begins to work in my life . . ." so I guess that's kind of mystical.

Joel: I grew up Christian and still am, and I also grew up loving pop music or whatever, rock music, and I realized . . . about five years ago I wrote a book about this and as I was writing it, I realized that those two things were so connected for me, the idea of music as this kind of spiritual thing, as this kind of powerful, whatever. I just noticed that for me I almost couldn't separate my love and my attraction to music from my sense of, kind of, spirituality and how I experienced God.

I'm not trying to lead the question, but I know that for a lot of people, like me, there is a real connection between the arts or music or whatever and spirituality. Do you sense that in your own life? I guess it was a business that you did with Kill Rock Stars, but do you sense a connection there at all?

Slim: Now you said that thing about business right at the end, but I want to specify that I was really actually pretty crappy at trying to make money. The whole reason that we started that business was really to release records that I thought that the world needed to hear and to help my friends make money from their art so that they could live off of that, instead of having to have day jobs. We did end up making some money, but it really wasn't the plan.

Joel: I didn't mean to imply you were only in it for the money!

Slim: It's relevant, because the thing is, I thought music was so important. I thought music was so healing and transformative that I wanted to give it to the world and giving it to the world was more important to me than like moving up the job ladder or making more money or buying a car with my first middle-class income.

The thing is, music touches us in a way that is beyond verbal, and to get really mystical, it's like we're made—it's hard to figure out what evolutionary purpose our musicality serves, but we're clearly built to be made to really respond strongly to music. Not just to the big things like a drumbeat, but a very, very, very subtle piece of music would still have strong emotional responses.

Some of that is cultural, like I respond to different sounds than somebody who grew up in China, but it still seems universal that most humans are built to be very responsive to music. To me, that seems kind of mystical because it doesn't— I'm really interested in those things about humanity that don't make sense evolutionarily.

Joel: Absolutely, yeah. I think of music, language, the idea of love, the idea of worship, like, it's hard for me to separate those things sometimes because they seem superfluous to survival, right?

Slim: Exactly, yeah. Any church, any kind of organized worship setting that I've ever experienced has involved some music. Whether it's just the folks doing the worshiping, singing hymns, or whether there's a choir or some musicians, it's well-known that music primes people to be open and it's a really important part of the worship experience for most folks, at least in the Western world. I can't say for the whole world because I haven't really studied it.

I sometimes feel that certain kinds of music have gotten this reputation as being more holy than others, but that doesn't really hold up if you think about it, right? Why is choral music more holy than drone minimalism? To me, some music maybe opens people up more than others, but all music that continues to get made and has a listening audience clearly is opening people up to something that's beyond words and beyond . . . That just does seem mystical to me. Just the fact that you always have choirs in church is a strong testament to how important music is to spirituality.

Joel: In my world, popular music and religion are very entangled just because of the circle I grew up in and the scene that I was involved with. Have you encountered any of that? Outside of a worship context or church service context, have you encountered this melding of spirituality and music outside of church? I would go to Christian rock shows in the basement of churches in Spokane, where I grew up, and it was like, I would have these amazingly powerful—what I now feel are spiritual experiences that I wouldn't really feel when I went to church. Have you had any experiences like that, now that you've moved into this stage of your life?

Slim: No. Not so much, except—I've started to go to some Christian praise music shows, and I feel moved by some of the groups. I went to Hillsong, and I went to Bethel Music and Rend Collective. I really liked Rend Collective.

LAMENT

The pieces in this section all touch on a sense of lament: loss, emptiness, absence, and what takes the place of the things that go away. The first is about the closing of a Bible bookstore in a small town where I was living at the time. (It was one of several attempts to write *New Yorker* "Talk of the Town"-style pieces about the tiny town of Eureka, California.) The second is about Judee Sill, a cult singer-songwriter who played beautiful baroque-influenced Laurel Canyon folk in the 1970s but who died very young and left a kind of ghostly presence in her wake. The last piece is a feature about the band Modest Mouse and the way their songs are meaningfully about nothing, and what can be discerned from that absence at the center of their work.

Old Time Bible House

There's an almost tragic irony in a Bible bookstore closing its doors the day before Christmas Eve, but this was the position in which Cannon's Old Time Bible House on Wabash Street in Eureka found itself. The Bible House is what is usually called a Christian bookstore, the type of place where you can buy Bibles (naturally), Christian T-shirts and bumper stickers, books by the heavyweights of the evangelical world like James Dobson, T. D. Jakes, and Joyce Meyer, and most meaningfully to a handful of people like me, rock music by obscure Christian artists.

The eponymous Mr. Cannon, an easygoing, goateed man working the register, didn't seem in bad spirits on the second-to-last day of the store's existence. Clad in a T-shirt and jeans, he cheerfully recommended authors and gave advice about large-print Bibles to the few patrons who had managed to crowd into the retail space.

Even though the Old Time Bible House, a green, squarish building with bars on its windows, looks like a good-sized structure, passersby might not (as I didn't) realize that about 80 percent of the space is actually Living Water Pentecostal Church, where Cannon is pastor. The bookstore—at least in its everything-must-go incarnation—is tiny, and only about four people can shop comfortably. The inventory was nearly depleted, but as of its second-to-last day in business, one could still find the flagship books and CDs of evangelicalism in America that probably aren't available anywhere else within a hundred-mile radius (though a three-hour drive to Redding, home of the Pentecostal powerhouse

Bethel Church, would likely afford access to a treasure trove of the stuff). A copy of Hal Lindsey's apocalyptic-panic classic *The Late, Great Planet Earth* nestled next to C. S. Lewis's *The Lion, the Witch, and the Wardrobe.* The surprisingly hip music section included, alongside a few compilations with names like "Godrock," CDs and cassettes (Christian bookstores *always* have cassettes) by sophisticated, thoughtful artists like Rich Mullins, Kevin Max, and PFR. You could get an audio-drama version of *The Mark*, one of the popular Left Behind series, on CD.

According to Cannon, the shop had barely been breaking even for two years, and shutting it down will allow his church to add a room for kids. "I'd rather have a Sunday School classroom," he said.

It isn't as if Bibles will no longer be available in Eureka—there's always the Barnes & Noble at the mall—but there was a kind of gentle intimacy to the place that seems a loss. When I found myself a dollar short on my cassette purchase (Rich Mullins's *The Jesus Record*), the only other customer offered Cannon a bill on my behalf.

"I want to bless you," she said to one or both of us. But Cannon had already swiped my debit card. "Too late," he said. "It's OK."

Lord Have Mercy: The Songs and Life of Judee Sill

A musician dying young is an old, stupid, tragic, useless story, and it's made worse by the way we fetishize rather than mourn the lost. With all the nostalgia-driven reissues of artists both known and obscure, the tragedy is just part of the one-sheet from the record company, along with the press clips. *Look how unbelievably tragic this life was,* the press release demands: *the wheelchair, the drugs, the ex-wives; at least before he cut his wrists or jumped off the Golden Gate bridge or passed out in a gutter, he made a really interesting psychedelic punk-funk record for an unknown vanity label based in South Carolina.* This is how they get our attention, I know. It is our fault, too. I paid attention to the tragic press releases when they reissued Judee Sill's records, and I'm glad I did.

Judith Lynne Sill was born on October 7, 1944, and from there things get a little sketchy. The details of her biography remain vague—partly because she was never quite famous enough to warrant scrutiny during her lifetime, and partly because she was given to exaggeration in interviews. Did her first husband really die after shooting some rapids in a rubber raft while on LSD? Was she really the church organist in reform school, and did she attend it before or after robbing a 7-11 at gunpoint? Did she really dabble in occult religion? Was she bisexual? Did she get addicted to painkillers because of a car accident in which Danny Kaye rear-ended her? I don't know.

Conventional wisdom tells us that an artist's biography, strictly speaking, doesn't need to be dragged into an evaluation of their body of work, but we must note the stark contrast between the deliberately orchestrated melodic songs Sill recorded and her short, brutish, and nasty life, which ended at age thirty-five due to a cocaine and codeine overdose (the word "suicide" appears on her death certificate, though that's not entirely certain). It seems Judee Sill achieved in her music what she could not in her life: some degree of symmetry, of control, of peace.

One of the most remarkable things about Sill, other than her gorgeous music, is the unabashed concern for God in her lyrics. She was a singer/songwriter in the 1970s, the "one toke over the line, sweet Jesus" and "Spirit in the Sky" era of rock and roll, but her interest in God is more than passing. Not everyone agrees with me; I've scoured the archives of rock criticism and the internet's only Judee Sill email discussion list—it has only about three hundred and fifty members—and only come across a few debates about her religion. Some common interpretations: she was spiritual, but not religious; she wrote about Jesus as a metaphor for other things; her music was about connecting with the divine in all of us.

I'm fine with that—there are plenty of interpretations of the songs that seem pretty valid, and her lyrics do keep things a bit vague. Someone I discussed her with said they didn't hear anything remotely religious in her songs, and that there are no direct references to God. I disagree, but it also occurs to me that you don't need to make direct references to God when God is your world. And that, it seems to me, is what is reflected in the music of Judee Sill. She seemed to have an intimately mundane relationship with God; wherever she came down on matters of doctrine seems a distant and unimportant question. How else could you write these songs, how else could you speak this way? I can't think of a song of hers that *isn't* about spiritual matters.

Judee Sill's first self-titled album was released by Asylum Records (run by a young David Geffen) in 1971. Her music was fairly conventional for the time (though it strikes my ears as fresh, a bright acoustic guitar overlaid with layers of Sill's smooth pure vocals and touches of pedal steel) and the first track, "Crayon Angels," finds her "waitin' for God and a train / to the astral plane." "The astral plane" is one of those obnoxious hippie things that

I'm glad I missed out on as a child of the eighties, but it's clear that Sill's music from the get-go was going to be about searching for God. And not only *waiting*, for that implies a kind of passive hope that eventually God will show himself, some measure of agnostic thumb-drumming while anticipating a guest who might have stood you up. Sill's relationship with God is deeper than that, which we see on "The Lamb Ran Away with the Crown" (a reference, she once said, to "the dish ran away with the spoon," but with a bit more gravitas). "Once a demon lived in my brow," Sill sings matter-of-factly, and it's not hard to read her own addictions into a lyric like that. The song portrays its speaker as preparing to fight the forces of darkness, drawing a sword like the disciple preparing to slice off an ear, facing down serpents and devils. In the end, she sings, "I laughed so hard I cried / and the lamb ran away with the crown." *As if the battle was mine to begin with!*, she seems to have discovered. *What a joke!* This Lamb absconds, having secured the victory. The battle belongs to the Lord, as the Catholic folk musician John Michael Talbot sang.

Sill's second album, *Heart Food* is just as God-haunted, from the gospelly "There's a Rugged Road" to the final track, "The Donor." A couple of critics have mentioned that there is no mention of just who this Donor is (the title's motif runs through the album, which also has songs called "The Kiss," "The Pearl," "The Vigilante," and "The Phoenix"), but by now I suppose you can guess Who I think it is. There could be a relationship between the record's title and this track, which is, as Sill once said in concert, written to "musically induce God into giving us all a break." Jesus is a kind of organ donor, offering up a transplant of his Sacred Heart—as food, as the Eucharist, even.

Even if Sill had never made any other music, "The Donor" would be her legacy. It is, like a lot of Sill's songs, a masterpiece of desire and yearning. The introduction is a gorgeous mishmash of multitracked vocals (all Sill's, though they sound something like magic dwarves) doing a sort of medieval chant ("Kyrie eleison"— Lord have mercy) building to a climax—and then they all back off, and Sill is alone. What she seems to be singing about is her

own life, her art, her soul: "Songs from so deep / while I'm sleepin'
/ seep in." What agonizing beauty. The idea seems to be that the
songwriter, whether it's due to her mental demons or in spite of
them, has been given a supreme gift, a muse that allows her to
write beautiful melodies. And yet there is "an echo aching"—an
absence of God, perhaps, that she longs for.

"Your wake is wide," Sill later sings. Never have I heard such
a simple and devastating lyric about the divine. It is as if we are
rowing a small wooden boat on the ocean late at night behind an
enormous ship. No lights are visible, but we continue in its wake,
even if we are tossed about. The ship is making waves and we are
trying to understand the meaning of these ripples in our lives. All
we can do when we are confronted with such enormity is to ask
"leave us not forsaken." As the liturgical prayers say: Lord, have
mercy. Christ, have mercy.

After releasing her two albums, Judee Sill died. She did not
become important, pop-culture-wise, until the early twenty-first
century, when Rhino reissued those records, and as interest grew,
Water Records released a posthumous collection of her demos,
masterfully remixed by Jim O'Rourke, and a collection of her
live performances on BBC radio (many of which are redundant,
though it is glorious to hear Sill perform "The Kiss," no matter
how similar the recordings are). The most recent addition to the
Sill revival is *Crayon Angels*, a compilation released in September
2009 by the record label American Dust.

That Judee Sill could have lived such a seemingly short and
painful life and have made such music of comfort, joy, and peace
seems tragically miraculous, though surely we know it has been
done before by people as tormented as she was—Beethoven deaf,
Schumann suicidal, Schubert mad with syphilis. Sill's music was
about God, but she lived a hard life and died of a drug overdose.
Are there "lessons" we can learn here? What would we find? That
you can make what looks like beautiful and holy art in service to
the Creator, and still end up dead in your apartment at age thirty-
five? That saying bad things about David Geffen will stall your
career and you'll get in a car accident that will end up turning you

back on to heroin? These are too glib, and certainly not universally applicable. I listen to Judee Sill and it is nearly impossible for me not to come to the conclusion that all music is made, as Bach wrote on his manuscripts, *ad majorem Dei gloriam*, for the greater glory of God. You might disagree with me, and that's cool. But try if you will, just try to make music for some other reason and it will betray you as it strains toward heaven.

Ripping through Flesh, Wailing

Modest Mouse's Isaac Brock writes a lot of songs that are not particularly about anything. They are shambling sketches of muddled
lives, in which the best thing that can happen is that nothing particularly bad happens. Think of the band's two mega-singles, "Float
On" and "Dashboard," triumphant pop gems which celebrate
nothing more than muddling through. The crux of both songs is
a kind of broken celebration: Life is shit, but hey, at least it's life.

This is why the band's 2009 music video for the song "King
Rat," directed by the late Heath Ledger, feels like an awkward addition to the Modest Mouse canon. Ledger was a budding director
when he died, and he'd just completed the concept for the video for
the single, a song recorded for their last full-length, *We Were Dead
Before the Ship Even Sank*, but relegated to the B-side of "Dashboard" and later included on an EP collection of sundries called
No One's First, and You're Next.

The "King Rat" video uses Brock's unhinged celebration of
failure ("And you know you know you know it all went wrong") as
the soundtrack to a film with an explicit, didactic purpose—it's an
anti-whaling video. The video is visually gorgeous, rendered as a
kind of minimalist faux-animation, but its heavy-handed, obvious
message (hey man, what if, like, the *whales* were hunting the *humans*?) simply doesn't feel right for "King Rat," or for any Modest
Mouse song, for that matter. Brock's songs are purposeful in their
purposelessness, excavations of emptiness and loss that don't seem
to stand for anything bigger than themselves, and somehow generate their power from this very thing.

A strange irony of the "King Rat" video, whether or not you applaud the depiction of cartoon humans being skinned in service to a political point, is that the record it comes from actually includes a track called "The Whale Song." Why that song wasn't a natural choice for a video about whales isn't clear—maybe Ledger or the people who finished the video didn't know about it—but it wouldn't have been a better choice for a political message about whaling, because Modest Mouse is not an ideological band. Regardless of any political opinions the band members themselves might have, the music of Modest Mouse is a tribute to chaos, not causes.

"The Whale Song" is full of the anarchic bendy-guitar lines that have always typified Brock's songs, whether Brock or Dann Gallucci or Johnny Marr is playing them. (Marr joined the band for *We Were Dead*, which seems incredible, like if Keith Richards had somehow been in Green Day for a year.) The riffs are less pop hook than brain-worm, and a minute or so into "The Whale Song," the jumpy melody gives way to screeching and howling—a languorous moan that is even, yes, a little whale-songish. When Brock's vocals finally come in, he's once again singing about unfulfilled possibility: "I know I was a scout / I should've found a way out," he groans. Again, this would work better on a literal, *this-is-about-whales* level: one can imagine a member of the pod (whales travel in these family groups for protection, right?) watching the others succumb to nets and spears before he himself is caught ("I'm rising up / wish I was sinking down").

But even this is too simple. "The Whale Song," the real plight of real sea mammals notwithstanding, is not a message-song; it's not about ecology or animal rights. It's another document (like so many of Brock's) of the human mess, of how we are trapped in and by ourselves and each other, how we do the things we don't want to do and don't do the things we want to do. As a metaphor, whales are pretty heavy-handed. Ask Jonah or Ahab or Pinocchio: They are always something big, something ominous and dark, something that will swallow us all, from which there rarely seems to be an escape. No redemption comes in "The Whale Song," no floating on, no melted radios playing summer jams: just those guitars, sound ripping the air like harpoons through flesh, wailing.

HOPE

Politics in the Republican/Democrat sense do not really interest me, but put a punk rock band screaming about hope, love, and justice in my ears and I will sign your petition. These pieces are all in some way about hope, revolution, and small-p politics. Most of the bands mentioned here are Canadian, but all the pieces were first written before I moved to Canada. Go figure. The first is about the Dears' EP *Protest* which I heard not long after I was in college and trying to figure out whether you can have a 9-to-5 and be an activist. The next is about the Stars album *Set Yourself On Fire*, one of my all-time favorite records and one that helped set me on the path to writing about religious resonances in decidedly non-religious pop music. The piece about dance music was published by the radical Canadian Christian magazine *Geez* and was very fun to write even though I have probably never actually danced to that music. Finally, I have written many pieces about the Weakerthans (for my money, one of the greatest bands of all time) over the years, and this one explains what I find so compelling about them, while also attempting to elucidate what "rocking out" really means.

The Dears: Protest

> Anyone who talks about revolution and class struggle without
> referring explicitly to everyday life—without grasping what is
> subversive about love and positive in the refusal of constraints—
> has a corpse in his mouth.
>
> —RAOUL VANEIGEM, *THE REVOLUTION OF EVERYDAY LIFE*

I can speak the language of the vaguely anarchist dilettante. I too,
attended a liberal arts university, read Marx and Engels, voted
Nader, and joined the window-smashers at the WTO protests in
Seattle in 1999. (Not that I smashed windows. I was just there.)
But like my friend Daniel said before he dropped out, college is
a fantasy world, a place where people get together and think they
can change the world by circulating petitions and growing beards.
It's great while you're there: somebody tells you that the world
would be better if all those idiots could be bothered to care about
whatever cause they believe in, and then you believe in the cause
and work on it and look down on people who don't, and feel good
about yourself. That didn't work well for me once I finished college
(even though I still work at one), and I now prefer Martin Luther
King's "love ethic," one that respects everybody, that doesn't hate,
and that protests not for the sake of protest, but for the sake of
actually changing wrong into right.

That makes me sound a lot more like a hippie than I intended. A Canadian neo-hippie-new-wave-Britpop band called Stars

put up a version of the above quote from the situationist Raoul Vaneigem on their website some years ago, though it was slightly altered and attributed to the British post-punk musician Pete Wy-lie. When I first heard the *Protest* EP by the Dears, I immediately thought of it, since the Dears and Stars are both from the same music scene, Canadian kindred spirits. I am trying to figure out if the Dears have corpses in their mouths or not, given the vaguely Marxist vibe of these songs. Somehow, I am thinking they do not.

The slowly building, menacing, and slightly Soviet first movement, "Heaven, Have Mercy On Us," is an invocation, a re-peated mantra (just the song's title, over and over) that gets things started. Though the initial organ riff could be straight from the Streets' "Let's Push Things Forward," the epic sound they're going for works. And it works because they're humble. This isn't the righteous indignation of a Rage Against the Machine—it's the sound (a big ol' choir, too) of a people who know their world is going to hell and know they're part of the problem.

Then the beat gets moving, and it's a transition into the "Summer of Protest," a nice little pop number to get people fired up to protest . . . something. (The anger seems to be directed at "every dollar that kills," which ranks high on the list of good things to be angry with. I should note that this EP came out in 2002, long before the resurgence of mainstream political protest in North America.) It skips along nicely, though it trips my pacifist radar with lines like "force we will use!" Still, they've got such a nice, languid melody going, and the instrumentation is sad and pretty, reverby and gloomy, and when a man and a woman sing in unison "start up a revolution / revolution for fools," it feels good and right, like "the soft revolution" that those hippies from Stars are always talking about.

Right after that the Dears start screaming the word "Revolu-tion," there's a siren sound, and things get pretty repetitive, until the siren turns into a guitar. Thankfully, the final movement is a lovely little piano ballad that is the contemplative foil to its (pi-ous and righteous, respectively) predecessors. "No Hope Before Destruction" is slow and mournful, and is concerned with a lot of small words that represent big ideas: hope, love, trust, fun, peace, light. It is possible to pigeonhole these as the concerns of sensitive glasses- and sweater-wearers who like to read books by Catholics and Quakers and Buddhist authors, but speaking as one of those people, I think these might be the most important things in the world, literally matters of life and death, and they do feel like things that have been slowly eroding for far too long.

And I don't know if these guys read the *Left Behind* books,[1] but "No Hope" almost seems like one of those "end times" things, the singer sadly declaring that there will be "no hope / before / destruction." A lonely little snare drum and that communist chorus from the first song punctuate this song of resignation. Thankfully, we are not told that destruction is inevitable, simply that hope, like the other litany of good things they mention, will end before the big end comes. It is the end of hope, I take it, which we should be protesting the most fervently.

---

1. Tim LaHaye and Terry B. Jenkins; Tyndale, 1997–2005.

There is Only One Thing:
Stars and the Soft Revolution

Sometimes, while I'm busy reverse-baptizing all my favorite music in an ideological "everything is sacred!" frenzy, I have to ask myself: I wonder what these bands would think if they knew that they make me believe in God? With Stars, I actually got to find out. After I wrote a version of this piece about their album Set Yourself On Fire, *Torquil Campbell, the band's fey, engaging front man, posted this short message on the website of the publication: "This is the most interesting review of our work I have ever read. Am I a Christian without knowing it? Somewhere, my Anglican grandmother is smiling." Two other writers for alt-weeklies went on to quote my piece to the band in interviews, so I guess it made something of a mark, but honestly, I'd write an article like this about almost every band I love, in a heartbeat.*

Pop-culture-engaged Christians love to claim things as our own. From *The Matrix* to *The Simpsons* to Radiohead, if it's not altogether evil—if it's at least "vaguely Jesusy," to use Anne Lamott's phrase[1]—we will somehow squeeze and twist a thing until it is almost Christian. So let me be the first to claim the Canadian pop band Stars as my favorite drug-using, sex-having, love-promoting, totally non-Christian Christian band ever. They may be hedonistic, poppy, sentimental, political, and occasionally just goofy, but

---

1. Lamott, *Small Victories*, 191.

100

I cannot write this band off for a simple reason: a sincere and exhilarating love radiates from everything Stars puts out. And it's all kinds of love: sexual, spiritual, platonic, even something approaching that elusive *agape*.

The band's very name should give us a clue: they are not *the* Stars. As Torquil Campbell sometimes reminds the band's audiences, "We are stars and so are you." This is more literal than figurative: Anglican priest and scientist John Polkinghorne, in *Quarks, Chaos, and Christianity,* reminds us that "every atom of carbon inside our bodies was once inside a star. We are all made from the ashes of dead stars."[2] There's more to this oneness of humanity than just our physical makeup, and Stars sings about it all: the big stuff like sex and death and smaller details like high-school reunions and shared taxi rides.

The band is in the habit of beginning albums with thesis-statement-like epigraphs. Their first LP, *Nightsongs*, begins with a spoken quote from the poet Charles Baudelaire's "Invitation to the Voyage," which is translated "all is order and beauty, luxury, peace, and pleasure." *Nightsongs* was sexy and hungover, an album about looking for love in bars, deserted city streets, and painful memories. There's an electro-pop slickness to the album and its successor, *The Comeback* EP.

The 2003 album *Heart* starts with each band member earnestly stating his or her intentions: "I am [name], and this is my Heart." The first track, "What the Snowball Learned about Love," is a tender song about a curious cat watching its owners make love. The whole record is wonderfully alive to the possibilities of romance, its apex being the soaring "Elevator Love Letter," a joyous assurance that there's something much better—the arms of the beloved—waiting for the downtrodden cubicle drone at the end of the day.

Set Yourself On Fire, which was released in 2004, starts with a more dramatic pronouncement: "When there's nothing left to burn, you have to set yourself on fire." This sets up a grander vision for Stars and concretizes the manifesto of what the band calls

2. Polkinghorne, *Quarks, Chaos and Christianity*, 29.

"the soft revolution," which, I daresay, is something Christians might do well to be a part of. The personal is the political, goes the old progressive slogan, and on *Set Yourself On Fire* it is difficult to separate the personal from the political, or for that matter, the religious from the political, the sexual from the religious, or the infinitesimal from the infinite. This is not to say that Stars thrives on contraries; their philosophy is more all-encompassing (remember that carbon) than paradoxical.

The best distillation of the album may be the title track, which is partly a reference to the practice of Buddhist self-immolation, a suicidal gesture which, as Charles Orzech writes in his essay "Provoked Suicide," is "meant as a creative, constructive, and salvific act . . . intended to remake the world for the better of everyone in it."[3] The title can also be a metaphorical call to become fully awake and alive to the possibilities of life and love—the way evangelical Christians talk about being "on fire for the Lord."

The repeated mantra of the chorus, "there is only one THING" (emphasis in the original liner notes),[4] over a frenetic, driving bass line, then, can easily be taken as a reference to a Buddhist-influenced monism: the song is a litany of people, places, and things; from "a cancer ward where the patients sit / waiting patiently to die" to "inside your lover's head," all is one.

But I must confess I hear something a little less Buddhist in these lines. In my head, the idea expressed in this chorus goes on for much longer: I follow "there is only one thing" with something like "only one thing that matters, anyway, and that one thing is Love, and that Love is embodied in Christ, and Christ's Love envelops and sustains us, and we should reflect that same Love to envelop and sustain one another."

The rest of the album, too, is full of love, and it spills out everywhere. Most of the songs feel like small miracles, from the tired sensuality of "Sleep Tonight" to the subdued celebration of "Calendar Girl." "Ageless Beauty" may be Stars' tightest pop song yet, and it is characteristically bursting with hope: Amy Millan

3. Orzech, "Provoked Suicide," 158.
4. Stars, *Set Yourself On Fire* (liner notes).

sings "We will always be a light" (again, my brain continues, ". . . for hope, love, joy, peace, patience, truth, justice. . .") and asks the listener to "loosen your heart." "What I'm Trying to Say" is sweet without being saccharine: what I'm trying to say, as it turns out, is simply "I love you."

Nobody is gentle and loving all the time, of course, and "He Lied About Death" is a downright vicious attack on George W. Bush. But why do they hate him? Certainly because of his war, but also, notably, what Campbell and Millan perceive as his replacement of love with fear. "You scare the love out of here," they chastise. The song closes with a blistering, screeching, two-minute instrumental section that is as danceable as it is angry. Frustrated by the seeming impotence of political protest, Stars opts simply to make music in the face of fascism and oppression.

What is "the soft revolution," then? The lyrics to the song offer clues, and in them again are echoes of the Gospel. Campbell promises: "We are here to make you feel / it terrifies you, but it's real." Some years later, in an interview with *Vice* magazine, Campbell would elaborate on this:

> My dad taught me that in art everything must always go wrong. Losing is the human condition. We lose together and we win alone. You should never, ever fight battles that you are not certain you are going to lose because if you are only fighting battles that you are certain you will win you're a fucking fascist. Winning is for fascists, man! Winning is for Donald Trump. And losing is for the rest of us. Winning is an illusion and loss is real. The price of love is that you say goodbye. I just always believed in loss and that if people showed more weakness in the world we could beat the bastards.[5]

It's hard not to read this and think of Christ's strange and revolutionary inversion of worldly power, of turning meekness into strength, of defeating death by willingly submitting to it. Stars is no more a Christian band than, say, the Beatles or Aerosmith, but when I listen to them, my heartstrings vibrate. This is why I

5. Campbell, "Rank Your Records" (interview).

will keep recommending their music to people who care about the things I believe God cares about, the things Christ teaches. I will warn them that they'll be wading through drugs and sex and death and war and hate on these records, but what they'll find at the end is hope, faith, and always, always love.

Dance Dance Revolution

"If God is a DJ," begins P!nk's 2006 single, "God is a DJ"—and if you buy this first premise, apparently "life is a dance floor / love is the rhythm, you are the music." In the song's final seconds, the Almighty's plan for our lives (Jer 29:11 notwithstanding) is revealed: "God wants you to shake your ass." Corny, but that sentiment is the driving force behind a weirdly compelling trend in music, an ass-shaking Great Awakening led by a disparate trinity of flamboyant dance acts that are, in some way or another, propelled by Christianity. And while they might not admit to being part of a movement—other than the electric slide—Seattle's United State of Electronica (U.S.E.), Atlanta's Family Force Five (FF5), and Paris's Justice are all saying the same thing: dance music is nothing short of a sanctified revolution, and if we'd all just do what P!nk says God wants, the world would be a better place.

There's always been spirituality where there's dance, but no band has exploited it like ("secular") French duo Justice, who appropriate the most Christian symbol imaginable: the cross itself. It's the name of their first album (simply rendered †), and is displayed at their concerts more prominently than any Christian rock band could dream of: huge, neon, blazing. Like most dance acts, Justice brings high energy and positivity, but the presence of the cross lends gravitas to the grooves. Unlike Christian bands, Justice isn't getting funky for Jesus; they're getting funky in a world presided over by Him, on instrumental tracks like "Genesis," "Let There Be Light," and "Waters of Nazareth." The room with the house beats is also, somehow, a house of God. And the movement starts here.

If the dance dance revolution has a manifesto, it's a track on U.S.E.'s self-titled album, a spoken proclamation which calls on "people who wanna shake it and raise their fists" to join "a true revolution in music—not as retaliation, but as an acceptance of all sounds and all people." Armed with sugary synth-vocoder, constant 4/4 drumbeat, sequined tank tops, and up-with-people positivity, U.S.E. was formed by a nucleus of musicians who met at Seattle Pacific University, a Christian college, in the 1990s. Their self-titled album is a celebration of such heady theological topics as dancing, love, fun, parties, *beach* parties, love, music, and love. Dave Segal followed the band on a Japanese tour for Seattle's alt-weekly the *Stranger*: before U.S.E.'s biggest shows ever, they chant a group prayer in unison (something they do before every show, Segal writes), after which their front man Noah Weaver shouts, "Let's fuck shit up!"[1] What U.S.E. does is, they fuck shit up for the Lord. They don't *mention* the Lord, but if you listen to the lyrics behind the vocoder—"let the love light shine," "music is love," "I can show you the way under the umbrella of love," "I got more love than anyone could ever wish for"—it's clear: Love will save the world.

Family Force Five also believe this, with an unbridled enthusiasm: their sophomore record, released August 2008, is called *Dance or Die*, and they really are *that* serious, despite the absurd haircuts and flashy mashup of southern rap, nu-metal, and dance-rock. The band's "big break" beyond the Contemporary Christian Music ghetto (where they had a home with Gotee records), was their "Love Addict" music video, which blends 80s buttrock tropes (hot chicks in hot pants, headbanging, ridiculous lipstick) with devotion to an ambiguous "love," which is "sent from above." FF5's singer, whose preposterous (and somehow spiritually significant?) pseudonym is Soul Glow Activatur, quakes like a man possessed in the video, which, frankly, he is. Single-minded and obsessed, nearly every FF5 song is about love, or dancing, or love of dancing, and how all of this stuff is more important than anything else. The basic message, delivered with breathless urgency, is "HEY EVERY-BODY WE ARE PART OF SOME KIND OF HUGE AWESOME

1. Segal, "Rising Sun."

THING!!" For FF5 there's no doubt that the awesome thing is God, who moves in not-so-mysterious ways through breakdancing and getting crunk.

There you have it: three bands of full-grown adults jumping up and down in service of a truth we've known since the Beatles: "love is good." They're not saying "God is good," or even "social change for the sake of a more just world is good." But come on: love *is good*. The dance dance revolution may be glittery and spandexy, but it may save the world—or at least get you to obey that still small voice telling you to move your booty. That's the first step.

Rocking Out with the Weakerthans

Every once in a while, I get to thinking how frustrated I am with not having time to make music; as an academic I do too much reading and writing and teaching to have time to sit down with a guitar and make stuff up, let alone join a band. I was in rock bands for a decade before I started grad school and my academic career, and I miss it. I started thinking about why, although I enjoyed the things I was doing in my academic career (mostly related to writing and language), I felt like something was missing. So I came up with this thing I called the Theory of Rocking Out in order to explain why I was pining for rock music when I was engaged with academic pursuits. The Theory of Rocking Out is this:

> Playing in a rock band is a supremely satisfying physical, emotional, intellectual, and spiritual experience of meaning-making, way more so than reading and writing about theories.

Which is kind of, like, *duh*, I know. When I told a friend about it, he replied, "that's not a theory, that's a *law*."

By "rocking out" I mean making meaning, perceiving and understanding with body and soul, throwing oneself into the creation of sound, song, story. Usually this involves sweating profusely, breaking guitar strings, and drinking a lot of beer. There's just something about making sense of the world through the form of a three-minute song combining the best of poetry, propaganda, technology, and bare feeling; it's meaning with body and multimodality, being in the world via sound and story, living the questions by asserting oneself bodily and narratively.

When I think of the Theory of Rocking Out I think of the Weakerthans, a pop-rock band from Winnipeg, Manitoba, led by self-proclaimed "talk-singing sober leftist vegetarian Quaker" John K. Samson.[1] Their music has offered me an antidote to academia for many years, a way of exploring things that matter without overthinking them, applying premade "theories," or analyzing them to death. Those things are, among others, love, community, relationships, thanksgiving, tenderness, and a hunger for justice. These things are everywhere in the music of the Weakerthans.

"Plea from a Cat Named Virtute," from their 2003 album *Reconstruction Site* is what first hooked me, a pop song verging on punk—oh the clarion call of those trebly bass guitar lines!—with the most sympathetic of lyrics: a pep talk, delivered by a cat, to her depressed owner. "I know you're strong," she purrs. What really slays me is the next track on the album, "Our Retired Explorer (Dines with Michel Foucault in Paris, 1961)." With one deft song clocking in at 2:25, the Weakerthans present a convincing dismissal of the ugly, unuseful side of academia—it's a song of art over theory, story over analysis, passion over examination. The song is true to the implications of its title: an explorer, one who traveled to Antarctica with Ernest Shackleton, meets post-everything philosopher Michel Foucault. From the second line of the song, the difference between the two becomes pretty clear: "I'm not entirely sure what you're talking about," sings the explorer.

What's inspiring about the character in this song is the way he immediately launches into a litany of things he must do (feed his dogs, commandeer a ship) to get back to his true love, the iciest continent (the song ends with a repeated chorus of "Oh Antarctica!"), which is of course representative of quite a bit more than a continent. It's the Big Story, abandoning the minutiae of "reason" for the pursuit of love. He trips all over himself to explain to the philosopher the sheer beauty of the place. Samson gives the explorer the tenderest lines of adoration ever spoken in praise of a chunk of ice.

1. Samson, "About."

Samson takes the concerns of his characters like the explorer seriously, without making them caricatures, and the kindness and care—the genuine love—with which he gives them voices and bodies, even when they are pitiful or pitiable, is remarkable. The ruined businessman of "Relative Surplus Value," the washed-up curling hero-turned-barfly of "Tournament of Hearts," even a runaway housecat on *Reunion Tour*'s saddest song (a sequel to "Plea from a Cat Named Virtute")—all of these characters would be punchlines to a less charitable lyricist, but in Samson's hands they are beautiful and fragile and believable.

Somehow, taken together, the little vignettes Samson sings about and the band so touchingly plays (and the way their records are recorded! they sound exquisite), about hospital prayers, a pamphleteer ignored by passersby, and P. G. Wodehouse novels left behind, present a picture of life so much more appealing than one lived in the nervous light of the laptop waiting for reviews of that new journal article. What I'm talking about here is nothing more, really, than four Canadian dudes devoting a lot of time and energy to communicating one mundane fact: *Being human is pretty remarkable.* But we so rarely take the time to acknowledge this amid the bureaucracy and posturing and deadline-missing of academia. It is right and necessary to be reminded: Being human *is* pretty remarkable.

TRANSCENDENCE

As somebody who mostly writes about rock and roll, I've always found it difficult to write about instrumental music, even though I enjoy listening to it. The pieces in this section are about how to discern meaning in music that is ostensibly somewhere in the pop/rock world, but that has more in common with other non-pop genres, or has no lyrics, or sometimes, even, no melody. Somehow, this is music that transcends lyrics, that *means* beyond words in ways that are not immediately clear. I've been trying to understand how this is possible, and these three pieces are my attempts. The first is my exploration of the mysterious "genre" (if you can call it that) of drone music by listening to it, interviewing people who make it, and attempting to make it myself (as usual, with a more competent musician pulling more weight). The second, in a similar vein, examines "post-rock" music and its embrace in spiritual settings. Finally, there is a short piece about the album *The Lemon of Pink* by the band the Books, which looks at sound collage in the light of language teaching and learning (which happens to be my academic specialty).

Perfect Sound Forever

Play a sound
with the certainty
that you have an infinite amount of time and space

—From the score of Karlheinz Stockhausen's
improvisational instrumental piece
"Unbegrenzt" (Unlimited)

Intuitively, I feel like music should *move*. It should take advantage of polyphonic possibilities, be catchy, and make you want to dance or sing or nod your head. In the modern world, we are accustomed to music as an emotionally and spiritually cathartic thing, and it can be an overt guide and shaper of our experience. I'd know less about love if I'd never heard Peter Gabriel's "In Your Eyes," and faith if I'd never sung "Come Thou Fount of Every Blessing." Melodies and lyrics combine in ways that seem to open us up to meaning, moving us in ways neither can on their own.

But there is a kind of music that lacks both lyrics and melody, that largely lacks movement. This is the drone: a single note, played for a very long time. Drones have been used around the world for years, and traditionally they function as a sort of baseline against which a melody can be played. Think of the wheeze of a bagpipe, or the sitar-like buzz of the *tanpura* in Indian *rāga* (or the Beatles' "Tomorrow Never Knows"). In historical Christian music, there's the *ison* of Byzantine devotional chant, a low, sung bass note as the rich backdrop for the rest of the piece. The pedal bass notes of a church pipe organ function in a similar way.

There's something seemingly sacred about drones; as Australian journalist David Rutledge wrote, they have "a transcendent, hypnotic quality that under the right conditions can elicit a meditative or even religious response. For those inclined to do so, it's not difficult to hear God in a drone."[1] In traditional contexts, the drone is the anchor for a piece of music, the rock upon which a melody can be built. Rutledge interviewed the early music scholar Winsome Evans, who said a drone on a tonic (the first note of a scale) represents "the One," in other words, "the Godhead," and "it's from that One that the melody evolves."[2] The drone signals rootedness of all meaning in God's presence, the work of the Creator sustaining creation.

Modern drone music, too, is linked to divinity and eternality. In the 1960s, composers like Karlheinz Stockhausen and La Monte Young seemed to attribute a deep spirituality to sustained notes, and many contemporary ambient music artists don't bother with building melody on that mystical foundation. The emphasis is more on creating sustained sounds, and the feeling of the drone standing for something much bigger remains. Stockhausen wrote a series of pieces (*Aus den sieben Tagen*) which direct performers to simply play sounds for as long as they want or can, and to consider the cosmological implications of infinity. Young formed an improvisational group, the Theatre of Eternal Music, that played hours-long pieces based on drones.

There's something of intentionality and slowness to this music compared to the pop and rock music that provides a backdrop for many of our lives, and that seems to open listeners up to transcendence in ways other music does not.

I first heard about drones because of rock music, though. *Mercury*, the 1995 album by the Christian indie rock band the Prayer Chain, opens with the ethereal "Humb," built around a formless guitar drone created by engineer Chris Colbert. It doesn't sound like a guitar at all, though. It sounds like . . . I don't know, an ocean?

1. Rutledge, "Drone Music."
2. Rutledge, "Drone Music."

A forest? It's a beautiful sound, and one that got me interested in the spiritual possibilities afforded of drones: What is the potential of this kind of music for expressing the kind of awe and wonder we feel in the presence of God?

A friend and onetime bandmate of mine, Kevin Scott Davis, records ambient and post-rock/neo-classical music under the names Glowworm and Beta Cicadae. I asked Kevin whether he thought there was any connection between drone and ambient music and Christian spirituality. "Centering prayer often uses a short single phrase ('Christ is love,' et cetera), repeated as a tool to come back to a place of focus in Christian mysticism, like the mantra *ohm* in Eastern meditation," he told me. "I think drone has an analogous musical effect."

I got a similar response from Jesse Eubanks, who runs the Christian social justice ministry Love Thy Neighborhood in Louisville, Kentucky, and who has also recorded several ambient pieces that incorporate drones: "I think drones offer a special invitation to the listener," he said. "God is infinite and unchanging. Drones are about timelessness. They don't focus on the question of 'What's going to happen next?' and instead focus on 'What exists now?' They are like musical breath prayers. They can be an aid to being mindful to the presence of God—to practicing meditative prayer and contemplative Scripture reading. Sonically speaking, by the nature of their form, they help us in quieting the outside world and our own anxieties and hearing the still small voice."

This was all appealing. Like many of my generation, even though I've played and sung them for years, the pop-style "worship" songs I hear in evangelical churches on Sunday mornings are much less compelling to me than they used to be, and I often feel a yearning to try something different, musically, for worship. So I decided to actually do it.

I persuaded my pastor to let me use the sanctuary of the Anglican church our congregation was renting for a couple of hours one night. I asked my friend Matt Smith, who is a great pianist and has a cool synthesizer, to come along. We decided to play in the key of C—in fact, to play mostly just the note C, and add improvised flourishes as we saw fit. I brought a bass guitar, which I leaned against an amplifier for most of the night, letting the feedback do what it would—mostly creating a long, loud hum. Matt turned up the reverb and the delay on his synth, holding chords for minutes at a time. We did this for about ninety minutes, Matt playing triads and single notes on the synth, me fiddling with the volume knobs on the bass amp, trying to control the timbre of the tones.

This was meant as a musical and spiritual experiment, to see what we could do with drones, and also if drones would "do" anything to us, or to the church. I was too focused on trying to create sounds to feel like I was doing anything close to prayer or meditation the way Kevin and Jesse talked about, but when I listen to the recordings, I can imagine, I do believe, that something unique happened.

I started to figure this out when I asked my friend Hedy Law, who is a musicologist at the University of British Columbia, what she thinks happens when drones are used for religious purposes. She talked about how religious music (especially in chants or drones or other hypnotic, repetitive forms) is an interpersonal experience—a group of people allow themselves to be taken to a sublime space together. "You can't just play a drone," and expect it to be spiritual, she said. "It cannot be coerced. It has to be something very deliberate in order for that religious experience to happen."

I asked her, then, what she thought happened when we played those long, sustained sounds in the church that night. She responded with another question: "What did you want to do?"

She explained that you can use a drone to create a religious space, but the religious experience is intersubjective. The experience of sonically transforming a space can only be understood in relation to some other space or experience. By attempting to change the sound in a religious space, you can suggest a different spiritual experience, perhaps. What did I want to do? My goal of filling the sanctuary with drones, feedback, and ambient noise was in part a reaction to the music I hear on Sunday mornings. The whole notion of slowness, patience, and timelessness is opposite not only to most modern church music, but to most of the pop or jazz or classical or folk music we listen to every day. I wanted to try something slower, more focused and contemplative. I also wanted to take advantage of the acoustic possibilities in the space. I spent years hiding behind a plexiglass shield as a drummer in church bands, because churches are not built for rock music, and the cymbals would overpower everything. But I *wanted* to fill the empty space with sound.

What we played was nothing like a Sunday morning rendition of "Blessed Be Your Name"—not something better or worse, but utterly different. No choruses, no verses, no words, just tones ringing out in an empty space. There was a stillness and a solemnity in the room I rarely feel on Sunday mornings—especially now that the Anglican church has been torn down to make way for apartment buildings and our church is back to meeting in an elementary school gym.

Drones don't *make* timelessness or eternity or God, of course, but they can, I think, sonically shape a space—shape us—in ways that make us more attuned to these mysteries. And this music that is different from what most of us know, that's *supposed* to not move, begins to feel like something other than music, almost: something otherworldly, outside of time, and even holy.

Groans Too Deep

"Does it sock you in the gut? Does it buckle your knees? Does it take your breath away?" These are the questions Marc Byrd asks himself when he writes music for his band, Hammock.[1]

Chances are that you've heard "God of Wonders," a song Byrd co-wrote, at church. But you may not know his labor of love, Hammock, which has released two full-length albums of blissfully atmospheric melodies and almost entirely no lyrics. Composed of Byrd and Andrew Thompson, Hammock writes spacious songs full of echoes and spacey keyboards, and sometimes features ethereal vocals from Byrd's wife, Christine Glass, and lush cello accompaniment from Matt Slocum of Sixpence None the Richer.

Hammock belongs to the genre loosely known as *post-rock*. With deep roots in independent rock music (some trace it to the 1960s), post-rock has emerged in the last ten years as a phenomenon typified by bands like Sigur Rós, Mogwai, Godspeed You! Black Emperor, and Explosions in the Sky (whose music is the opening theme for the now-classic TV series *Friday Night Lights*). While these bands use rock instruments and the occasional horn or string section, they have more in common with classical music, building long, symphonic compositions with swelling emotional climaxes.

Post-rock is increasingly being made and used by people of faith both inside and outside church contexts, reflecting a stylistic and ideological move away from praise choruses and toward

1. Unless otherwise cited, the quotations in this section are all from personal correspondence and interviews.

instrumental music as a vehicle for praise and reflecting God's glory.

"I do think the current move in many Christian circles toward post-rock is a trend that seems to mimic a bit of the influx of post-modernism," said Brent Thomas, then a teaching pastor at Grace Community Church in Glen Rose, Texas, who often discusses post-rock bands on his blog. "The open, expansive nature of the music reflects the more open, expansive nature of God that many are trying to regain after so many years of systematic theology."

The Icelandic band Sigur Rós, whose blend of neoclassical composition, soaring guitars, and often wordless vocals has in no small way influenced the current move toward post-rock in Christian circles. Unless you've heard them, it may seem coun-terintuitive that a Scandinavian band with pagan leanings and a gay lead singer whose lyrics are sometimes made-up syllables with no distinct meaning would be so influential in American Chris-tian circles. But there's an overwhelming sense of awe present in Sigur Rós's music that has captured a generation of religious rock musicians.

"The world is charged with the grandeur of God," Gerard Manley Hopkins once wrote,[2] and Sigur Rós compositions like "I Gaer," are charged with that same grandeur. Starting with a modest glockenspiel melody, the song suddenly cracks open like a raging electrical storm, a billowing frenzy of guitars and drums. The band is often joined live and on record by the string quartet Amiina, and together, the musicians build songs of such epic scope that it seems only breathless hyperbole and metaphor feel suitable as an explanation: the music sounds like angels dancing, birds soaring above clouds, flyover shots of glaciers. There's such a hugeness to the band's songs, a slow, patient unfolding in service of something more than entertainment or selling albums. Sigur Rós understands how to create space for listeners to experience songs. This is true both because of the long moments of profound stillness in their music, and the openness with which their lyrics can be interpret-ed. They aren't singing about that maddeningly vague "something

2. Hopkins, "God's Grandeur."

more" that Christian bands like to hide behind; in fact, it's hard to understand whether they're singing about anything at all, and sometimes they're not. While many of Jónsi's lyrics are in Icelandic, some are also in a wordless vocal style he calls "Vonlenska" (usually translated as "Hopelandic").

There's been a lot of hype about this "language," but perhaps it's close to what St. Paul had in mind when he wrote of "groans too deep for words."[3] The lyrics to "Vaka" sound something like: "ee-sai-a-lo, ee-so / ee-saw-ee-slow, ee-so / . . . you-shy-naw-no-ee-oh." What does that mean, exactly? "You saw the light?" "He saw you low?" "You shine on us?" Something entirely different? Combine these vocals with the band's aptitude for reverent, hymn-like songs, and you'll see why Sigur Rós became a template for a certain kind of Christian music.

"I went to a Sigur Rós concert in LA once that changed my life," said Eric Owyoung of the band Future of Forestry. "I felt the depths of God's beauty in those songs." Formerly in the more pop-oriented worship band Something Like Silas, Owyoung now makes music with an ear for epic soundscapes and mystery: "An environment of beautiful music simply awakens the innermost part of us and brings us to places of awakening and communion with God."

Claes Strängberg, founder of Swedish post-rock band Immanu El, describes his own music as "atmospheric, beautiful, and unsettled," which goes a long way in articulating the genre that's beginning to capture a generation's spiritual longing.

"This music is what I do, and that is also me," Strängberg said. "To me it is the ultimate expression for my faith."

***

Dissatisfied both with Seattle's independent music scene and contemporary worship music, Zadok Wartes had a vision for something grander. That vision became Urban Hymnal, a

---

3. Rom. 8:26.

quarterly worship service held at rotating locations whose music relies on the tropes of the post-rock genre.

"Our culture has become so fast-paced that it's exhausting, and along comes music that's restful and slow and doesn't give you your fix in four minutes," Wartes said. "When we're doing Urban Hymnal stuff, we unabashedly want things to be beautiful, making the music longer and slower. And we talk about patience and waiting and slowly arriving somewhere. To really draw someone into an emotional arc, we feel like it takes six, seven, eight minutes, not four."

The group takes an approach to church music that goes beyond using instruments as mere accompaniment for praise lyrics; they instead create moods, an atmosphere of reverence. The Urban Hymnal song "Love Is Fear" features several minutes of vocalist Tara Ward "singing in tongues," says Wartes. "Tara's part comes in and it's just ethereal. I can get lost in it."

These bands aim to offer an opportunity for the co-creation of a worship experience shared by listener, performer, and Spirit alike, whether it's due to the wide-open feel of the instrumental music or the presence of vocals in Hopelandic, Latin (Future of Forestry's "Sanctitatis"), or glossolalia.

"There's nothing wrong with praising God in word form," said Justin Shepherd of the instrumental band Foxhole. "It's a major part of our Christian heritage. But there's more to give to God than praise. There's also something valuable in reflecting on him, and not him only, but on his Creation and his children and his Enemy and all that comes with that."

Foxhole's *Push/Pull* EP, inspired by a real life tragedy, follows an arc of "the dying, death, and rising up of our friend," said Shepherd. On the potential for spiritual expression through instrumental rock, Shepherd said: "I think it falls into that realm Paul talks about, the 'groans too deep for words,' where you are struggling to stay upright without clear discernment of where you're headed or what you're to be doing."

These groans—whether in the form of wordless vocals, the squall of trumpets, or the endless feedback loop of an electric guitar—can invite listeners to long for communion with God.

But the freedom afforded by post-rock is that it's often made without a particular agenda. It's not made to persuade nonbelievers or instruct the faithful. It's music that aims to usher listeners into the presence of beauty, mystery, and the divine.

"When this music is playing, it does something to make [people] sit back and soak in things that are around them that they might take for granted," Hammock's Byrd said. "I want to put some beauty out there in the world."

The Lemon of Pink

She is one of my best students, but she is shaking—involuntarily, almost imperceptibly shaking, tiny twitches of her hands and lips as she tries to do what she, like almost all of the four hundred college students I teach in this medium-sized university in this medium-sized town on the east coast of China, is here to do: speak English. To a real live foreigner. A terrifying prospect. It isn't easy, having a conversation in a foreign language: your tongue and teeth connect in unfamiliar, uncomfortable ways, and you feel like a bit of an impostor, forming words that do not feel like yours.

To put together a coherent sentence is a battle—a battle made more difficult by the years of English exams they've taken, teaching them to shoot for grammatical perfection—and a battle punctuated with guttural sounds. *Uh, um, en, nèi ge,* sharp intakes of breath, sighs, grunts, groans. It's all here.

And it is all here on an album by a band called the Books. The album is *The Lemon of Pink*, which already makes me think of my students (they ask me if I have seen the Disney film *The King of Lion*, for example), but it is the record as a whole that says so much about the process of learning a language, of trying to speak strange syllables.

This album doesn't have much in the way of lyrics, and in fact you'd be hard-pressed to call some of these tracks "songs." For example, "Explanation Mark" contains the "lyrics," "ah ah, oh oh, oo oo, ha ha, ha ha, ho ho, ho ho, hu hu, hu hu, he he, oo ha, oo ha, oo ha," which seem to be taken from a recording for people trying to practice vowel sounds in a new language. The whole thing inhabits a very tentative linguistic and ideological space, which is just the sort of space my students and I inhabit when we try to talk to each other here.

China is hardly a monolingual place—the hundred-some "dialects" that are spoken here are often mutually unintelligible, and sometimes you can't understand somebody who was born the next county over. This album inhabits an in-between space, the way a lot of people learning languages in today's world do. China is not Singapore, that is to say, it is not a place where English, though originally "foreign," is a necessary and oft-used tool for communication; but it is a place where anybody who is anybody is learning English, and if you are a foreigner here you are trying (probably halfheartedly) to learn Chinese, so you are all grasping for anything you can find in common—shared sounds (you may be relieved to find that "oh" means basically the same thing in Chinese and English), body language, belief.

Perhaps we cannot say that the spark of hope and seeking of a new way of understanding that guides the acquisition of another language is the same that leads people along on their spiritual paths, but the two seem to mingle on *The Lemon of Pink*—amid the barely coherent syllables, the foreign languages snatching here and there, you'll hear faint snatches of faith—out of the pastiche of singing, sounds of family vacation, and cello, The Lord's Prayer emerges in a lilting Middle English at the end of "S is for Evrysing," bringing some peace and closure.

My favorite track, "Take Time," chops up the book of Ecclesiastes, cuts up the verses the Byrds used for "Turn! Turn! Turn!" and reminds us that "that which is now and that which is to be hath already been." All this learning we are doing to try to communicate to each other has been done for centuries before us. *Take time*, the persistent chorus sings. *Take time*.

I say this to my students, to myself. It can be really depressing when the only thing you really know how to say in your new language is your name and where you are from. But take time. After all the breathing, all the shaking, all the learning, all the time, you'll have done something real and human. It will be worth it. Take time.

SELF

A popular sentence you see on many people's social media bios: "Opinions my own." This is presumably meant to inoculate one's employer against being held responsible for one's inflammatory internet ramblings. I've never used the phrase, because if I'm honest I have no idea whether my opinions are my own or not. I hardly know anything about myself—whether I am serious or goofy, whether I'm especially kind or a huge jerk, whether I'm smart or completely lack common sense. As Walker Percy writes in *Lost in the Cosmos*: "A stranger approaching you in the street will in a second's glance see you whole, size you up, place you in a way in which you cannot and never will, even though you have spent a lifetime with yourself, live in the Century of the Self, and therefore ought to know yourself best of all."[1]

This section includes pieces dealing with the self in some way, but they're all sort of travel writing pieces, too. (Travel writing itself is usually autobiography.) I wrote about my trip to England way back in the year 2000, which is one of the first pieces of "music writing" I ever did; a somewhat traditional music journalism piece that is a profile of, and interview with, the musician James Singleton, who is from my hometown of Spokane, Washington, written for Spokane's alt-weekly the *Inlander* but filed from Shanghai; and finally, a short piece I wrote about getting ready to move for graduate school.

---

1. Percy, *Lost in the Cosmos*, 7–8.

Invisible Balloon

In the film adaptation of Nick Hornby's *High Fidelity*, record store owner and pop music obsessive Rob Gordon comes to the conclusion that what truly matters about people is "what you like, not what you are like. Books, records, films, these things matter."[1] I don't think I believe this, but there was a time when I lived as if I did, which means I have a valid excuse for having spent my two-month study abroad sojourn in the United Kingdom at the turn of the century doing nothing but looking for record stores. Other twenty-year-olds might have taken advantage of the situation by getting shitfaced every night (a not insignificant minority of my study-abroad classmates went this route); the more high-minded might have pursued museums, historical landmarks, and literary sites of interest. I, however, spent sixty days looking for discount book and music shops, spending most of my meager budget on music magazines, CDs, and rock concerts.

Part of me regrets this, and feels even now that I should have been more excited about seeing Blake manuscripts and Matisse paintings than finally finding some Smiths albums at a decent price (even considering the exchange rate). Maybe my priorities were simply askew; I had been lured away from true beauty and "high art" by a crude imitation wrapped in a cheap, faux-fur coat and wearing too much makeup. Even if this is true, I came to terms long ago with my deep, irrational love for pop music, and I don't regret the way I've made it a central part of my life. Searching for

1. Frears, *High Fidelity*, 57:56—58:04.

and purchasing popular music recordings was my primary mission in life from roughly age fourteen to twenty-seven, with the England trip occurring at the apex of this phase. From the moment I stepped off the plane, whether my trip would be defined by my insatiable quest for good albums, my hunger to see interesting concerts, and my unending hunt for bargain CDs was not even a question. It was inevitable. Like the start of the U2 documentary *U2: Rattle and Hum*, I resigned myself to the fact that this would be, as Larry Mullen Jr. says in his lilting accent, "a musical journey."[2]

My trip to England was bookended by two significant cultural events in the UK, namely the death of the Queen Mother at age 101, and Queen Elizabeth II's Golden Jubilee. (And perhaps more importantly, the twenty-fifth anniversary of the release of the Sex Pistols' incendiary "God Save the Queen" single, possibly the most controversial piece of music released in Britain's history. Unthinkably, the single was reissued on CD and LP with the B-side being a "dance remix" of the punk classic.) Music was always there, though, whether the sounds of newly crowned British "Pop Idol" Will Young in the background at a coffee shop, Oasis performing at "Top of the Pops" on my host family's television or an English garage band on stage in front of me, playing curiously American-sounding rock and roll.

It's impossible for me to remember all the details of the music I experienced in Britain. A handful of images stand out: I saw an American musician, Ben Kweller, whose guitarist was too drunk to play. I went to a concert at the Bath International Music Festival, where rain poured on us for two hours while we watched musicians from Africa, India, and South America, and I saw two women kiss each other for the first time in my life. I saw a teenage punk band celebrate the death of the Queen Mother and the demise of "what she stood for—fascist monarchy and superficial Christian morality." ("She was a hundred and one!" a concertgoer shouted back in a sort of feeble defense of the royal family, or at least kindness to the elderly.) I sat in the back of a dark London basement (the deceptively named Notting Hill Arts Club) and saw—or couldn't

2. Mullen Jr., quoted in Joanou, *Rattle and Hum*.

see—an indie rock band cover Guns N' Roses and Yo La Tengo songs. I met some Japanese exchange students who liked Weezer. I sang Oasis' "Wonderwall" and Gorillaz's "Clint Eastwood" at karaoke. A comedian made fun of me from the stage when I told him my favorite band ("If you want to kill yourself in the next six months, keep listening to Radiohead"). In Liverpool, I met a man who said he'd seen the Beatles dozens of times, then I drank a beer and saw a show at the Cavern Club, which was nearly a religious experience.

My main goal for March to May in the two thousandth year of our Lord was to find one CD in particular, a kind of power-pop Holy Grail I'd been tracking since high school: an album called *Jukebox* by the band Midget. (It's OK if you haven't heard of them; most people haven't.) I knew one song by the band, a single called "Invisible Balloon" that I had heard on a compilation CD released by a US magazine sometime in 1997. The song is absolutely *exquisite* pop-rock, a joyous stack of melodies, harmonies, distortion, and upbeat backing vocals, like the Beatles meets Blur meets Elton John meets Ben Folds Five meets Green Day. Technically, the internet existed, but it was not yet the sole destination for finding and listening to music—it was still normal to simply search for physical copies of albums. And search I did.

The first major CD-shopping excursion (with Midget on my mind and one hundred pounds in my pocket) I made was in London, and I spent nearly five hours walking around Berwick Street, which according to my copy of *Time Out London* had a "genuinely seedy feel." Indeed, the assortment of shady-looking vendors juggling soccer balls, used CD and record stores, tiny restaurants, and cramped cafes lent the area a certain "quaint" (dodgy) ambiance. The presence of a long string of sex shops at the end of the street and a drunk middle-aged man propositioning passing women upped the seediness quotient.

My search for *Jukebox* and other musical bargains took me to every music store on Berwick, and each was full of clerks who had no recollection of the single, the album, or even the band. Nevertheless, the outing was enjoyable and educational, and not just for the thrill of pursuit. I was forced to come to terms with the fact that my habit of scouring the "discount" bins for my favorite obscure bands would not be an option, since I hadn't even heard *of*, let alone heard, any of England's truly obscure indie bands.

As I walked into the delightfully named Mr. CD, I immediately headed downstairs after noticing the sign pointing to the "bargain basement." (I noticed later that this was common among CD shops I encountered. It took me a while to realize why practically every independent music shop in England had a bargain basement or attic. It's because England is built that way: lots of small, narrow rooms stacked on top of each other.) In the basement of Mr. CD, I felt as if I'd walked into a scene in *High Fidelity* (not the Chicago-based movie, but the book, set in London). Two middle-aged men in leather jackets were scrutinizing a wall of albums, muttering comments to each other like "have you heard this one yet?," "their first album was brilliant," and "they were popular in the States." Their rapid-fire exchanges and vast knowledge of bands I'd never heard of made me wary of even opening my mouth in a music store in Britain; I was afraid my accent would belie my musical knowledge. One word would give me away as the ultimate brainless American: thick Southern accent, complete ignorance about all things British, and prone to statements like "*Hah. Ah am not frum around heeyar. Do you hayuv the re-kord ah am looking for? Mah fay-vor-ite john-ruh is kun-tree and way-us-turn.*"

The clerk at Mr. CD humored me as I attempted to explain who Midget was, and even claimed to have a vague recollection of a band matching the limited description I gave him (mid-90s, energetic, upbeat Britpop, which surely defined dozens of bands). Nevertheless, he didn't have it. I purchased an album by British band Hefner for two pounds, thanked him and moved on.

I also came up empty-handed at Reckless Records, a bigger shop with a large selection of American "Indie Rock," which, although it is short for "Independent Rock," basically meant, at the time at least, "music that most people haven't heard of and which sounds like it was recorded in a bathroom." I couldn't help feeling a little superior as I noticed patrons eyeing Built to Spill or Pavement albums. I wanted to take some of them aside and say, "Hey, I *live* in the place all these bands are from. I've seen those guys live! Twice!"

As I left Reckless, I considered my status as a Seattle hipster among London hipsters. I felt I had credibility thanks to my home being the birthplace of a significant genre and one of the world's most important rock bands (grunge and Nirvana, respectively), and I saw plenty of records by Pacific Northwest bands on the shelves in the UK. I became convinced that my country (or even my city) had invented the culture I saw around me at British music stores and concerts, and that their version was a poor imitation. Occasionally I even caught myself believing the kids I saw at concerts to be copying *my* personal "style," never mind that my Converse were in storage in Seattle and my retro, thrift-store jacket was hung in my closet at home.

By the end of the day, my tired, Converse-less feet had carried me up and down Berwick and even to England's largest HMV and Tower Records Piccadilly (also England's largest). All I had to show for it was the Hefner CD, which I didn't really like all that much, and the knowledge that Midget had released another album in 1999 which was available, but *Jukebox* was, as the ominous British music-retail lingo puts it, "deleted."

Still, there was a chance that someone had bought the album long ago, hated it, and traded it in for a Spice Girls CD or something. I remained optimistic as my search broadened to used CD shops in other localities, but things weren't much better outside London. A short weekend trip to Scotland proved worse, at least as far as the helpfulness of the proprietors I encountered, both of whom apparently had better things to do than assist customers.

While wandering the streets of Edinburgh, I noticed a few signs advertising a record store. The cramped shop was full of boxes of records stacked one on top of the other, a few racks of CDs arranged in no particular order, and barely enough room to turn around. I managed to bring up the subject of Midget with the owner, but didn't even have a chance to blurt out the band's name before I was dismissed by "We only do blues and jazz, I don't know anything about that." Here's a haughty Scotsman, I thought, peddling genres that wouldn't exist if it weren't for the US of A, and he won't even take a moment to help me. Even more insulting was that the store obviously sold more than jazz and blues; the dregs of American and British rock were liberally spread throughout his used CD section. I left suspecting I had fallen victim to a Scottish xenophobe and hoping my bulging backpack would knock over a stack of Rolling Stones albums.

The next Scottish shop owner was hardly more courteous. He was clearly more "with it," stocking the latest rock releases, but when I mentioned Midget (I was able to recite my entire spiel, which I had memorized by this point) and that I believed their albums were somewhat hard to find, at least in the US, he proceeded to lecture me on the travails of being a record store owner. "Two hundred albums come out every week," he said with the weight of the pop music world on his shoulders, "multiply that by months, and by years . . ." He went on to make it clear that it was impossible for him to keep track of just every band that released an album. I wanted to explain that (a) as not only a fan but the music director of a university's radio station and a music journalist, I was fully aware of the volume of music that exists in and is always entering the world, and (b) that I wasn't asking him to recite, on the spot, every album that was released on September 16, 1997, or whatever; I just wanted to know if he knew anything about a cool band called Midget. I was angry, but not angry enough not to buy a rare Portishead single from him before I left.

Scotland was proving as big a disappointment as its southern neighbor, Midget-wise. Thankfully, the nation musically redeemed itself in the form of a dimly lit pub whose name I have forgotten, but whose patrons I won't. While wandering Edinburgh in search of nightlife, my traveling companions and I came across a large, dark pub whose musical guest that night would be the Counterfeit Clash, a Clash tribute band. We elected to check out the pub, have a pint or two, and enjoy the music of one of England's great punk bands played by, we assumed, some middle-aged Scottish hacks.

The concert itself took place in a small, concrete-walled room with only two tables and a handful of chairs, so this was clearly a *gig,* not just background music to ignore while socializing. The band tuned up and informed the audience (in what, to these American ears, was an utterly incomprehensible accent) that they would play one set of other bands' songs before playing a set of Clash covers. The band ripped through relatively faithful renditions of some tunes by the Specials, Madness, and even the Talking Heads' "Psycho Killer." It was pretty standard fare for a cover band; infinitely more interesting to watch than the musicians, to me, was their audience.

As more people arrived to hear the band, the room became increasingly damp, the air thick and humid with exhaled breath and perspiration. We were in what felt like an underground cave, and it was as if the walls themselves were sweating, the tiny room laboring to contain the exuberance of its occupants. I suppose this contributed to the almost primeval, proletarian unity the people in the room seemed to be enjoying. Everyone—the aging "original" punks, their demure, dressed up-girlfriends, and just the neighbors for whom this was their local—knew *all the words to all the songs*, and they belted them out at the tops of their lungs. There were innumerable groups of two or three singing in unison, arms around each other, fists or pints raised, dancing to the unofficial anthems of Britain. (Amazingly, even the most drunken and ardent fans of the band, joyously thrashing about in time to the music with no regard for dignity or safety, never spilled a drop of beer. This is something I have come to greatly admire about British people.)

The Scottish pub, and not my failing search for *Jukebox*, is the image from my trip that has been most firmly imprinted in my brain. There were museums and plays, and concerts, and there was history and beautiful countryside. But that loud, loutish celebra tion of life, the noise and solidarity and love that I saw in that room was something remarkable. I'd never seen such camaraderie, fellowship and sheer blue-collar solidarity. Whatever mystical amalgamation of elements was at work that night—maybe just cheap beer, punk rock hymns, and the beginning of the weekend—affected me more than any work of art I saw in the Tate Gallery or the British Museum.

After six weeks of searching, I finally found *Jukebox* at a shop in Bath. Upon hours of walking around the city and dutifully purchasing non-Midget albums (I can't pass up a good deal on a Britpop record, no matter the artist), I was exhausted, ready to go home and give up. I was absolutely elated to find the album, and I told the clerk so as I purchased it. He didn't share my enthusiasm, but I wasn't going to let anything get me down. Luckily my host family was out when I got home; I put the album on the stereo and it was just what I'd hoped: forty-two minutes of pure pop bliss. Every song seemed so instantly catchy that I could start singing along before it was finished. Every chorus was in the right place and repeated the right number of times; every note of every guitar solo resonated in the part of my brain that loves melody. I'd found the Grail.

My last night in England, I rode the London Eye, a sort of giant Ferris wheel operated by British Airways. From the top of the ride, the whole city of London is visible, and because it was the night of Queen Elizabeth's Golden Jubilee celebration, there were fireworks everywhere in the night sky. After two months of experiences that were about my interactions with the British on a micro-level—whether my disillusionment with their shop inventories or being squeezed up against them at rock shows—it was refreshing to disappear into the sky and observe the city at night. Fireworks flashed, Big Ben was lit up, and somewhere down there, Paul McCartney, Eric Clapton, and Phil Collins were playing at an enormous concert in honor of the Queen. It was huge, sprawling, bustling, and beautifully alive, and I was free to simply observe it from the top of the world.

It was there above all of London that those nonsensical pop lyrics made sense: "Be a king, be a queen, be anything / where you won't be seen," Midget sings. "When I'm up so high in the sky / no one sees my invisible balloon." Inane, catchy, disposable pop lyrics, maybe. But these things matter.

World Wide Pants

We're eating whole pigeons—wings, beaks, eyes, everything—and spicy donkey in a private room at a Shanghai restaurant called, inexplicably, "Kevin," while the promoters gossip about whether or not Cut Chemist is a vegetarian. Someone casually lights up a spliff, but the waitstaff don't seem to mind; then again, there's something shady about a Chinese restaurant that manages, as Kevin has, to run out of *rice*. But there are larger paradoxes to confront tonight. Like, why is a dude from Spokane about to play funk and boogie records in a bomb shelter not far from the place the world's most powerful Communist Party was formed?

As his musical act, James Pants, gets bigger, James Singleton's world is getting smaller. And crazier.

***

Joel: Graphically, I'm imagining a map with a little
             dot from Spokane, like, going out into the world.
             You've been in London, in France, now China—
             what has been your most positive international
             experience so far?

James: There's been a lot. But I will say the craziest, in
             terms of *crazy*, has been Moscow, Russia, like a
             month ago. I was on tour with my band. I had
             low expectations. I thought, who would have
             heard of me in Russia? My record label doesn't

have distribution in China or Russia. So, I just thought, "no one's going to know us." And it was in-*sane*. The promoter came up to us during the soundcheck, and he was like [exaggerated Russian accent] "So, what do you want for tonight?" And we were like, maybe twelve beers or something, because there were four of us. And he was like, "No, what do you want for tonight?" And we were like, well, maybe a bottle of vodka. And he was like, "We have seven backstage. What do you really want for tonight?" And so at that point we were thinking like, oh, God, what is he asking us here?

Joel: What, like, "What kind of girls do you like?"

James: Exactly. So, that kind of set the tone for the night. We started playing at three in the morning, and it was *packed* packed—*packed-packed* packed. People were insane. It was the biggest energy I've seen, ever. I remember going outside afterwards, and my bandmates were signing girls' breasts, and their passports, and I just thought: this is like total A-list treatment. It's like we're U2 or something. And we're just some podunk band. We play in all these "cool" cities, like London, New York—and nobody's half as good. But in Moscow, Russia, these people are insane. I think they're just really hungry for music, because they've been shut off for so long. I'm hoping tonight will be like that.

At the soundcheck, Singleton's manager, who is Chinese American, is surprised when I tell her my cab driver asked me about Obama's recent election. "They're allowed to know about that?"

Yeah—and sometimes they know it better than Americans. I've met thirteen-year-old Chinese kids who know more about the US government than I do. It's the same with pop music—students here listen to Linkin Park, Death Cab for Cutie, Metallica. "In China young people are more mainstream," said Al Di, an executive with Universal Music in Beijing, when I asked him if he thought Singleton's music would catch on in the Middle Kingdom. Universal makes bank selling Rihanna and Mariah Carey records, Di said, but in his estimation, "The time is not quite ready for indie musicians to come to China."

Indeed, a quick glimpse around the room at Eno, a Chinese clothing boutique where Singleton is doing an instore before the gig, doesn't suggest that the crowd are here because they dig super-underground hip-hop mashups. A few well-dressed Shanghainese yuppies are here, but there's a whole lotta English being spoken, which means there's a sizeable crew of what the Chinese call "foreigners" in attendance.

So, has Free the Wax, the scrappy Shanghai-based promo company and labor of love run by Brazilian Leo Messias and Chinese Australian Katrina Lui, truly brought James Pants "to China," or is he just here to entertain the international party people, a demographic with disposable income that will show up to see him spin wherever there's cultural capital to be spent and earned, at fashion shows in Paris, Urban Outfitters in New York, or the Apple store in Beijing?

Lui admits that the local audience usually doesn't "request anything more" than mainstream pop, but "we're trying to change it a bit, remind people that there is really good music out there. It's really important for us to get through to the Chinese people, but it's really difficult."

Messias has his theories on why under-the-radar music like James Pants hasn't caught on here—culture, language, even visual rhetoric (a lot of locals had trouble understanding the show's Chinese-language flyers, he said)—but ultimately it comes down to history, he says. "China missed out on the '60s and '70s. The references are limited. They're at a different point in history."

Plus, adds Gary Wang, co-owner of the Shelter, where Singleton is playing tonight, "the Chinese crowd comes really fucking early. Nine thirty they show up, there's no one there. And they leave at twelve thirty when the party just started."

The crowd at Eno sits, enjoys, appreciates—politely. Everyone's a little nervous about the show tonight. Who will be there? Will they like the music? We're a world away from Spokane's Baby Bar, the only place Singleton says he feels truly comfortable onstage.

***

Joel: A lot of your press materials, your bios and your interviews (even the ones with the English-language media in China) mention Spokane very prominently. Is that your doing, and if it is, why?

James: I think I did do a lot of that. I used to be embarrassed to say I lived there, and basically one day I woke up and said, "You know what, I live here, and strangely, I like it, and maybe it's an asset to start saying I'm from here, and not be embarrassed." Because, how many bands are from New York and LA? It's like "eh . . ." But there's no one from Spokane right now. I mean, there's bands there, but I think I'm the only one touring, really. It's just different; it differentiates you from everybody else. And I kind of embellish a little bit when I talk about Spokane. I like to create this picture of the weirdest place on earth.

Joel:	But why do you do that? I mean, I grew up there, and I don't really see it as weird at all.
James:	I think within the normalness, and suburbia, and the sheer poverty—it's a pretty poor town—it's like, "I can't believe this is here, this is so out of place." There's this thrift store I go to a lot on East Sprague called Drop Yer Drawers, and they come up with the weirdest keyboards. And they're so cheap. I bought a Crumar analog synth for twenty dollars. He said he sold a Moog the week before for fifty dollars, and it's just like "this is too good to be true!" Then I've been really into the Russian markets lately, and the Indian market. I think Spokane, it seems normal if you live in the suburbs, but it's a city where you create your own fun, and it can be a really strange place. To me, what fascinates me most about a city, it's not the downtown shopping—it's the weird corner stores that sell, like, used magazines or whatever. That's the stuff I love, and I think there's a lot of places like that in Spokane right now. It's a good place to be creative, I think.

***

It's getting on two in the morning, and everybody is bombed at the Shelter. Any worries about not drawing a crowd, Chinese or otherwise, were unfounded—the place is packed with locals, ex-pats, scenesters—there's even a girl from Texas here because she is genuinely a fan of James Pants. Singaporean beer is flowing, white dudes are trying to get dirty with Chinese girls, and a French guy is yelling at me not to publish any pictures of him. It's Friday night in Shanghai, a city that is working while you are asleep, staying awake to make sure you got the email, trying to avoid the lady whose job it is to shove you onto the Metro when it is already full on the commute home, and finally then partying its international guts out while Singleton grooves and grins away behind the decks, occasionally commandeering the microphone to accompany himself in falsetto or say "*xie xie*" to the crowd.

He's getting more comfortable. The crowd is on his side. Singleton plays a solo on a drum machine—using chopsticks—to wild applause. Requests start flying. The Beach Boys; "Don't Worry Baby," Diana Ross's version of "Ain't No Mountain High Enough," and a litany of other oldies seamlessly fly out of the speakers. Occasionally, Singleton mixes in his own music, which, I now notice, is usually just a few synth farts, a cowbell, and some vocal yowling. Everyone loves it. We are here in Shanghai, far from everywhere else in the world. Singleton is playing every song in the world. Everything is becoming a blur, moving forward. Back in Spokane it is still yesterday, and we are living in the future.

Static Waves

Camping at the southern tip of the Oregon coast years ago in late August, I woke early to walk along the beach and listen to Pacific UV's song "Static Waves" through my cheap headphones. The swirling, the fuzz, the reverb in my ears was joined by a real-life corollary: the fog that surrounded me, making it impossible to see more than a few dozen yards in any direction. I walked toward the ocean until I couldn't see where I'd come from, then picked another direction arbitrarily and set off. It didn't matter how far I'd gone or if I veered off course; every step took me into territory that was both completely unknown and totally familiar—I knew I would be surrounded by wet, white space, that my feet would meet the hard crust over the soft sand wherever they fell. Sometimes I walked with my eyes closed.

I was on my way to a new city, moving away from friends, from home, from the life I knew. Into something totally foreign, to a tiny town I knew nothing of, to attend a school I knew almost as little about. I was venturing into white space.

I walked and got lost; I listened to waves of guitar and wrote prayers in the sand with a stick. In the middle of all that nothing it was all I could think to do.

Then I went back to the tent and woke my wife up and we ate breakfast. Even now, though, it feels like I am still on the beach, in the white space among the static waves. The song reminds me that I am in the white space, we are all always in the white space, and we must learn to love it. I am trying, and some days I do.

(Coda: Silence)

(a found poem, spoken by Sufjan Stevens during an interview on
Radio New Zealand, January 23, 2016)[1]

Music is transcendent;
it's an invisible force.
It's an apparition of consequence;
sound waves that you can't see;

And I feel like that's kind of a representation of God.

Music is like the practice of faith, through song.
Music persuades us to believe in something we cannot see.

It offers meaning
and narrative
and consciousness
and hope
to something invisible.

It's a salve,
but it cannot really save us.
It can only accompany us on our journey
for a season.

1. Stevens, "Illness, Death and Faith" (interview), 16:56–17:54.

In some ways it's the evidence of God,
but it isn't God.

I believe that God is silence.

At the end of our lives there's this
sort of consuming silence, and we must
prepare ourselves for this:
the moment when all the sound
and the white noise
is subdued to nothing
and there's just this emptiness,
and from within this emptiness,
that's when we start
to hear the voice of God,
the infinite.

Till then,
there's so much
white noise.

Bibliography

Adorno, Theodor W. "On Popular Music." With the assistance of George Simpson. *Studies in Philosophy and Social Science* (The Institute of Social Research) 9 (1941) 17–48.

Agawu, Kofi. "The Challenge of Semiotics." In *Rethinking Music*, edited by Nicholas Cook and Mark Everist, 138–60. Oxford: Oxford University Press, 1999.

Aleshinskaya, Evgeniya. "Key Components of Musical Discourse Analysis." *Research in Language* 11 (2013) 423–44. .

Bakhtin, M. M. "The Problem of Speech Genres." In *Speech Genres and Other Late Essays*, translated by Vern W. McGee and edited by Caryl Emerson and Michael Holquist, 60–102. Austin: University of Texas Press, 1986.

Bazerman, Charles, and Paul Prior. "Introduction." In *What Writing Does and How It Does It: An Introduction to Analyzing Texts and Textual Practices*, edited by Charles Bazerman and Paul Prior, 1–10. Mahwah: Lawrence Erlbaum Associates, 2004.

Beaujon, Andrew. "Ironic Mind Meets Literal Mind." Talk at *Festival of Faith and Music*, March 2007. https://web.archive.org/web/20160821102159/ http://www.calvin.edu/admin/sao/festival/2007/audio/.

Benjamin, Walter. "One-Way Street." In *One-Way Street and Other Writings*, translated by Edmund Jephcott and Kingsley Shorter, 45–104. London: NLB, 1979.

———. "The Work of Art in the Age of Mechanical Reproduction." In *Illuminations: Essays and Reflections*, edited by Hannah Arendt and translated by Harry Zohn, 217–51. New York: Schocken, 2007.

Blitz, Jeffrey, dir. *The Office*. Season 5, episode 13, "Stress Relief." Aired February 1, 2009, on NBC.

Bozeman, Lee. "Thursday, November 21, 2013." http://www.leebozeman.com/.

Burke, Kenneth. *A Grammar of Motives*. Berkeley: University of California Press, 1969.

———. *Language as Symbolic Action: Essays on Life, Literature, and Method*. Berkeley: University of California Press, 1966.

Campbell, Torquil. "Stars Co-Frontperson Torquil Campbell Bluntly Ranks the Band's Eight Albums." Interview by Cam Lindsay. *Vice*, November 21,

2018. https://www.vice.com/en/article/59v3vk/rank-your-records-stars-torquil-campbell.

Chang, Ed. "Unbegrenzt." http://stockhausenspace.blogspot.com/2015/03/aus-den-sieben-tagen.html#Anchor%202.

Coltrane, John. Liner notes for *A Love Supreme*. Recorded December 9, 1964. Impulse! Records, 1965.

Danto, Arthur. "The Artworld." *Journal of Philosophy* 61 (1964) 571–84.

———. "The Transfiguration of the Commonplace." *Journal of Aesthetics and Art Criticism* 33 (1974) 139–48.

Fenner, David E. W. *Introducing Aesthetics*. Westport: Praeger, 2003.

Fish, Stanley. *Is There a Text in This Class? The Authority of Interpretive Communities*. Cambridge: Harvard University Press, 1980.

Frears, Stephen, dir. *High Fidelity*. Burbank, CA: Touchstone Pictures, 2000.

Frith, Simon. *Performing Rites: On the Value of Popular Music*. Cambridge: Harvard University Press, 1996.

Garofalo, Reebee. *Rockin' Out: Popular Music in the USA*. Boston: Allyn and Bacon, 1997.

Giacchino, Michael. *Ratatouille*. Burbank, CA: Walt Disney Studios, 2007.

Goldstein, Richard. "Giraffe Hunters." *The Village Voice* 12 (October 27, 1966). Quoted in Devon Powers, *Writing the Record: The Village Voice and the Birth of Rock Criticism*. Amherst: University of Massachusetts Press, 2013.

Goodwin, Andrew. "Sample and Hold: Pop Music in the Digital Age of Reproduction." *Critical Quarterly* 30 (1988) 34–49.

Gormely, Ian. "A Rivers Runs Through It." *Exclaim!*, October 6, 2014. https://exclaim.ca/music/article/weezer-rivers_runs_through_it.

Gracyk, Theodore. *Rhythm and Noise: An Aesthetics of Rock*. Durham: Duke University Press, 1996.

———. "Valuing and Evaluating Popular Music." *Journal of Aesthetics and Art Criticism* 57 (1999) 205–20.

H. K. M. "The Unseen World." *New Republic* 14 (1918) 63. Quoted in Garson O'Toole. "Writing About Music is Like Dancing About Architecture." https://quoteinvestigator.com/2010/11/08/writing-about-music/.

Haaland, Bret, dir. *Futurama*. Episode 72, "The Devil's Hands Are Idle Playthings." Aired August 10, 2003, on Fox.

Hayden, Ethan. *Sigur Rós's ( )*. New York: Bloomsbury Academic, 2014.

Heng Hartse, Joel. *Sects, Love, and Rock & Roll: My Life on Record*. Eugene, OR: Cascade, 2010.

Hopkins, Gerard Manley. "God's Grandeur." *Poetry Foundation*. https://www.poetryfoundation.org/poems/44395/gods-grandeur.

Horkheimer, Max, and Theodor W. Adorno. *Dialectic of Enlightenment: Philosophical Fragments*. Edited by Gunzelin Schmid Noerr and translated by Edmund Jephcott. Stanford: Stanford University Press, 2002.

Joanou, Phil, dir. *U2: Rattle and Hum*. Midnight Films, 1988.

Jones, Gaynor, and Jay Rahn. "Definitions of Popular Music: Recycled." *Journal of Aesthetic Education* 11 (1977) 72–92.

Keuss, Jeffrey F. *Your Neighbor's Hymnal: What Popular Music Teaches Us About Faith, Hope, and Love.* Eugene, OR: Cascade, 2011.

Klosterman, Chuck. *Eating the Dinosaur.* New York: Scribner, 2009.

Lamott, Anne. *Small Victories: Spotting Improbable Moments of Grace.* New York: Riverhead, 2014.

Llewelyn, John. *Margins of Religion: Between Kierkegaard and Derrida.* Bloomington: Indiana University Press, 2009.

Long, James. "O, To Be Rich." *CCM Magazine* 18 (November 1995).

McNutt, Ryan. "Back to the Shack: Did Weezer Change or Did We Change?" *Chart Attack* (October 7, 2014).

Meltzer, Richard. *The Aesthetics of Rock.* Boston: Da Capo, 1987.

Metacritic. "Illinois by Sufjan Stevens." https://www.metacritic.com/music/illinois/sufjan-stevens.

Mitchum, Rob. Review of *Make Believe* by Weezer. *Pitchfork*, May 8, 2005. https://pitchfork.com/reviews/albums/8614-make-believe/.

Morris, Chris. "Geffen's Modern Rock Methodology Pays Off." *Billboard* 106 (February 12, 1994).

O'Riley, Christopher. "OK O'Riley: Classical Pianist Christopher O'Riley Trades Rachmaninoff for Radiohead." Interview by Derek Richardson. *SF Gate*, September 11, 2003. https://www.sfgate.com/music/article/OK-O-Riley-Classical-pianist-Christopher-2590238.php.

Ong, Walter J. *Orality and Literacy: The Technologizing of the Word.* London: Routledge, 2002.

Operation Space Opera. Liner notes for *Songs from the Black Hole.* Released online, September 6, 2012.

Orzech, Charles. "'Provoked Suicide' and the Victim's Behavior: The Case of the Vietnamese Self-Immolators." In *Curing Violence: Essays on René Girard*, edited by Mark I. Wallace and Theophus H. Smith, 137–60. Sonoma: Polebridge, 1994.

Overstreet, Jeffrey. Reply to "Sufjan Stevens?!?" (forum post). *Arts & Faith*, April 19, 2004. http://artsandfaith.com/index.php?/topic/1823-sufjan-stevens-update-interesting-review/&tab=comments#comment-23012.

Owen, Spencer. Review of *Weezer (Green Album)* by Weezer. *Pitchfork*, May 14, 2001. https://pitchfork.com/reviews/albums/8611-weezer-green-album/.

Pattison, Louis. Review of *Volta* by Björk. *BBC*, May 9, 2007. https://www.bbc.co.uk/music/reviews/mwvr/.

Percy, Walker. *Lost in the Cosmos: The Last Self-Help Book.* New York: Farrar, Straus & Giroux, 1983.

Phillips, Arthur. "Dancing about Architecture: A Meditation on Possibly Futile Artistic Pursuits." *Believer* 64 (July 1, 2009). https://believermag.com/dancing-about-architecture/.

Polkinghorne, J. C. *Quarks, Chaos and Christianity: Questions to Science and Religion.* New York: The Crossroad, 1996.

Powers, Devon. *Writing the Record: The Village Voice and the Birth of Rock Criticism.* Amherst: University of Massachusetts Press, 2013.

Račić, Ladislav. "On the Aesthetics of Rock Music." *International Review of the Aesthetics and Sociology of Music* 12 (1981) 199–202.

Rutledge, David. "Monotony and the Sacred: A Brief History of Drone Music." *ABC*, May 6, 2015. https://www.abc.net.au/radionational/programs/earshot/monotony-and-the-sacred/6448906.

Samson, John K. "About." http://johnksamson.com/about.

Sanneh, Kelefa. "The Rap Against Rockism." *New York Times*, October 31, 2004. https://www.nytimes.com/2004/10/31/arts/music/the-rap-against-rockism.html.

Sawyer, R. Keith. *Group Creativity: Music, Theater, Collaboration.* Mahwah, Lawrence Erlbaum Associates, 2003.

Segal, Dave. "The Band of the Rising Sun." *Stranger*, April 14, 2005. https://www.thestranger.com/seattle/band-of-the-rising-sun/Content?oid=21044.

Stars. Liner notes for *Set Yourself On Fire*. Arts & Crafts, September 14, 2004.

Steiner, George. *Real Presences*. Chicago: University of Chicago Press, 1989.

Stevens, Sufjan. "Everyone Must Read Lewis Hyde's *The Gift*." https://sufjan.com/post/42039242933/everyone-must-read-lewis-hydes-the-gift.

———. "Pocket Full of Stars." Interview by kicking_k. *Plan B*, October/November 2005.

———. "Sufjan Stevens: Illness, Death and Faith." Interview by Kim Hill. *Radio New Zealand*, January 23, 2016. https://www.rnz.co.nz/national/programmes/saturday/audio/201786543/sufjan-stevens-illness,-death-and-faith.

———. "True Myth: A Conversation with Sufjan Stevens." Interview by Ryan Dombal. *Pitchfork*, February 16, 2015. https://pitchfork.com/features/interview/9595-true-myth-a-conversation-with-sufjan-stevens/.

———. "We All Come from Somewhere." https://sufjan.com/post/49371624155/we-all-come-from-somewhere-even-if-we-end-up.

———. Interview by Noel Murray. *A.V. Club*, July 13, 2005. https://www.avclub.com/sufjan-stevens-1798208555.

Vaneigem, Raoul. *The Revolution of Everyday Life*. Translated by Donald Nicholson-Smith. Oakland: PM, 2012.

Webb, Stephen H. "Can Christian Music be Real Rock and Roll?" Review of *The Lyre of Orpheus: Popular Music, the Sacred, and the Profane*, by Christopher Partridge. *First Things*, June 10, 2014. https://www.firstthings.com/web-exclusives/2014/06/can-christian-music-be-real-rock-and-roll.

Wilson, Carl. *Let's Talk about Love: Why Other People Have Such Bad Taste*. New York: Bloomsbury Academic, 2014.

Yorke, Thom. "Fridge Buzz Now." Interview by Dean Kuipers. *Ray Gun* 54 (March 1998).

CPSIA information can be obtained
at www.ICGtesting.com
Printed in the USA
LVHW112013281122
734203LV00005B/484

9 781498 293822